Praise for *Turning Rants Into Raves*

Randi and Carol use a storytelling tradition that goes back
thousands of years to help you teach your team the mechanics
of excellent service. Their characters Rant and Rave—combined
with the authors' 50-plus years of experience in service—will
help you laugh while you recognize service lapses that can
happen to the best of us, and then learn how to create great
customer experiences. Highly recommended!

> Rich Gallagher, author of the #1 customer service bestseller
> *What to Say to a Porcupine* and *The Customer Service Survival Kit*

Every business wants to deliver service that creates raving
customers. Unfortunately most muddle in mediocrity and
suffer the effects of ranting customers. Carol and Randi unlock
the five building blocks for achieving a customer-centric
organization. They provide actionable strategies to energize
employees, customers and ultimately your bottom line.

> Stan Phelps, author of
> *What's Your Purple Goldfish? How to Win
> Customers and Influence Word of Mouth*

In *Turning Rants into Raves*, Randi Busse and Carol Heady have
created an engaging, accessible customer service manual for
business owners and entrepreneurs. Using the characters "Rant"
and "Rave," the authors provide true-to-life examples of the
way great and not-so-great frontline service personnel think
and perform. They also include interviews with exceptional
service providers, weaving in specific tactics that can be used to
ensure your customers are treated like royalty. If you're buying
a customer service book this year, this one should be it.

> Lori Jo Vest, author of the customer service bestseller
> *Who's Your Gladys? How to Turn Even the Most
> Difficult Customer into Your Biggest Fan*

Customer service, as delivered by your employees, will make or break your business. Busse and Heady give you everything you need to know to keep customers for life from developing a strategy to getting your employees on board.

Robert Levin, Editor-in-chief and Publisher,
New York Enterprise Report

A spirited and colorful primer that reinforces the importance of customer service.

Micah Solomon, bestselling author,
High-Tech, High-Touch Customer Service

Turning Rants Into Raves hits a home run by taking you on a journey through real-life examples showing how the folks that you pay to attract and engage your valuable prospects and customers are actually chasing them away. It then does a very effective job of showing the reader how employees who are empowered, have clear expectations, and truly think like owners will actually, turn on your customers! This informative digest should be required reading for anyone dealing with customers, both external as well as internal.

Chris Westad
President, Morania Oil

We all know good and bad customer service when we experience it, but how do you define it, understand it and, most important, weave it into the culture of your organization? That's the trick. In this well-written, meticulously researched, and down-to-earth book, Carol and Randi reveal precisely how to transform our organizations into places where customer raves are the takeaways. It should be standard reading for anyone who takes business seriously.

Thomas P. Kruglinski
CEO, Adaptive Dynamics, LLC

What I love about this book is the story of how to engage with both your customers and your employees. Real-life examples of the little things that matter to make the customer experience memorable and to build loyal fans for your business. After reading this yourself, share it with your staff and your customers will see the difference.

Bill Atkins
Owner, Red Bank Limo

The tenets in this book will enable management of any sized enterprise to rethink how they provide products and services to their customers. Yes, the customer is king; however, Rant and Rave will remind you of the good, bad and ugly in how to deal with your customers. Required reading for all levels of management to be sure everyone in your company provides a customer experience that will lead to the Four Rs: Revenue, Retention, Referral and Reputation. Three Cheers to the authors!

Laura Sikorski
Director Customer Innovation and Optimization, Altivon

The book is very clear and cogent, and makes excellent sense. The "Four Rs" are keys to the success of most companies, and especially to those in the hospitality industry. We definitely need "owners"—not "renters". Thanks for helping to show that the path to a company's success is paved by happy loyal customers!

Steve Spencer
President, London Town Cars

Turning Rants into Raves lays out key customer service principles that every business should follow. By combining real life examples with a focus on the financial impact of distinctive customer service, Carol & Randi clearly demonstrate the need for exceptional service and how to achieve it in your business.

Brett Bohl, Owner
ScrubSquared, LLC

Customer service cuts across all businesses and professions. Concepts of loyalty and trust are indeed bolstered with exceptional customer service. This book is easy to read and clearly establishes what behaviors are needed to achieve customer AND employee success.

Angelo Pirozzi, Partner
Charles A. Barragato and Co. LLP

The content is easy to read, yet the concepts are not simple. As a small business owner, the exercises are spot-on and reinforce the material to give it relevance to my company.

Karen Perry
President, Event Journal, Inc.

You owe it to your business to get this book into all your employees' hands, regardless of their experience or whether they have direct contact with your customers.

Barbara Walters
President, The HR Advantage

What an easy read with meaningful impact! Every company would like to differentiate themselves with superior service. This book will not only show you what that looks like but will give you a straightforward path to get there.

Audrey Manchester
Vice President, Regional Sales Manager
Chemung Canal Trust Company

Customers almost never tell you when they are leaving, so you could be losing loads of money without even knowing it. In this book, Randi and Carol give you five simple mind shifts that will save you from those losses and will increase your repeat and referral business at the same time. By using these simple, low-cost, high-income techniques, watch your bottom line and your company morale increase instantly.

Dom Sutera
Director of Business Development
Academy Mortgage Corp.

This is a must read for anyone who wants to hold on to their customers and keep them for life.

Michael Capilets
Managing Director
SVAM International

Turning *Rants* Into **Raves**

Turn Your Customers On
Before They Turn On *YOU!*

By
Randi Busse & Carol Heady

Published by The Rant and Rave Company, Inc.
Hopewell Junction, NY

Copyright © 2012 The Rant and Rave Company, Inc.

ISBN Print: 978-0-9882395-0-0

This publication is designed to provide accurate and authoritative information in regard to subject matter covered. It is sold with the understanding that the publisher is not engaged in rendering legal, accounting, or other professional service. If legal advice or other expert assistance is required, the services of a competent professional person should be sought.

The Rant and Rave Company, Inc.
Hopewell Junction, NY
info@turningrantsintoraves.com

Ordering Information:
For ordering information or special discounts for bulk purchases, please contact the publisher at the e-mail address above.

Printed in the United States of America
First Edition

Acknowledgements

We have a number of people we'd like to thank for their assistance and support in making this book possible.

Our experiences and work with our clients played a major role in the development of our five principles, which are the heart and soul of the book.

The CEOs, business owners and senior executives who gave generously of their time to share their insights, experiences, and service philosophies added tremendous value to the book. The employees who graciously provided their perspective also were invaluable; their voices are often not represented, and including them allowed us to present a balanced viewpoint on the subject of customer service.

A special thanks to our creative team, illustrators Jay French and Patrick Ian Moss, who created Rant and Rave and helped us bring them to life.

Rich Khorigan provided encouragement, supportive feedback and chocolate chip pumpkin muffins, and our interns, Deana DeLisio and Kristen Morra, contributed their time to assist us with research and transcribing interviews.

We also thank our colleagues, friends and mentors, who supported us on this journey and those who provided feedback on the manuscript; you know who you are.

We are grateful to our families, who endured our constant chatter about a subject we're both quite passionate about.

And finally to each other, for the time we spent together over the last two years to give birth to this book. We couldn't have asked for a better collaboration of passion, experience, and dedication to improving the customer experience.

Table of Contents

Introduction

"They act as if I'm a bother and they're doing me a favor by dealing with me. I feel invisible and unimportant, as if all they want is to take my money and then have me disappear. Of course, they don't say it in so many words, but the vibes I pick up speak volumes. Here I am, spending my hard-earned money with them, and all I want is a smile, to be taken care of in a friendly, professional manner, and to be thanked for my business. Why can't I get that? I don't think I'm asking too much, do you?"

~

All too often, this is the type of comment we hear from friends, family and colleagues when they complain to us about their experiences as a customer. What are the chances *your* customers are describing their experiences with your company in the same way?

It turns out most customers either rant or rave about their experiences. As a manager, business owner or CEO, if you think you have no control over which way they go—ranting or raving—think again!

We don't have to ask you which type of reaction you'd prefer. The choice is obvious. No matter what industry, size, or type of organization you lead, delivering an experience that inspires your customers to rave is what every business wants.

Fortunately, you don't need a big budget, dedicated training staff or magic wand to get raves. All you need is desire and commitment...and our five principles in the hands of every employee who represents your company. Combining all three will help you provide experiences that will inspire your customers to rave about your company and allow you to earn their trust and long-term loyalty, which will positively affect your bottom line.

Our principles are presented throughout this book, along with insightful interviews with business owners and employees who consistently demonstrate outstanding customer service. We share illustrations depicting real customer service situations, good and bad, bringing levity to a serious subject. We also demonstrate the financial benefit of implementing our principles with data on the sad state of customer service—data that highlights the powerful effect customer service has on your organization's bottom line. You can apply what we share with you regardless of your industry or the size of your company.

Our mission—and the reason we wrote this book—is to help you create loyal customers who are inspired to rave about your company. Based on more than 50 years of combined experience in customer service within a broad range of industries, the work we've done with our clients and extensive research, we know customer experience is a leading predictor of customer loyalty. We've observed many businesses work tirelessly to earn that loyalty, yet they don't manage to create an overall experience that motivates customers to engage in long-term relationships.

It's a well-known fact that customer loyalty drives profitability and it's also common knowledge that it costs five times more to acquire a new customer than it does to retain an existing one. Acknowledging the direct relationship between customer experience and profitability, we've identified four business drivers that are linked to attracting and retaining loyal customers; we call them the Four Rs: revenue, retention, referrals and reputation.

We refer to these drivers throughout the book, noting that the experiences you and your employees provide to current and prospective customers will have a direct effect —positive or negative—on all four of them. In particular, we'll expose the monetary consequences that can result from substandard customer service.

We begin by introducing you to two very important fictitious employees, Rant and Rave, whose actions and behaviors represent the contrast between good and bad customer service. You have these types of employees working in your organization—and you may be surprised to learn about their behaviors and hear what they may be saying to your customers.

Think you don't have "customers"? It's really a matter of semantics. What do you call the people who do business with you? Throughout the book, when we refer to "customers," we mean the people you serve. You might call them clients, guests, students, patients, members, or something else; to us, they're your customers—and remember, you have employees like Rant and Rave serving them!

Throughout the book, we present our five principles and bring them to life through situations featuring Rant and Rave. Our intent is to encourage and motivate you to reflect on your own organization as you embark on a journey with Rant and Rave. Contemplate what you and your employees can be doing to inspire your customers to rave about your company.

Here are some questions you may want to start thinking about:

- When was the last time you spoke to your customers about their experiences with your company?

- Do you know how your customers feel about your company?

- What could you do differently to take better care of your customers?

- How does your customer service affect your bottom line?

To get the kind of business results you want, you must be committed to take better care of your customers, and ready, willing, and able to continuously improve their experiences with your company. Quality customer service requires relentless attention and an effective strategy that includes our five principles.

This book provides a "how-to approach," focusing on specific behaviors that will help you create loyal customers. Within each chapter, reflection exercises are provided to help you examine your actions and those of your employees, as well as your customer service policies and procedures. To maximize your success in turning rants into raves, we encourage you to complete the exercises as you read the chapters, and consider the practical strategies we've provided at the end of each one for implementing the five principles in your business.

There have been a lot of good books written on customer service and there's obviously more than one approach to delivering it in a memorable way. It's our intention that this book provides a fresh and unique perspective on how to deliver exceptional customer service that will inspire your customers to rave about your company.

Here's to turning your customers on before they turn on you!

Carol and Randi

The Journey Begins

"The goal as a company is to have customer service that is not just the best, but legendary."

Sam Walton, founder, Walmart

The Journey Begins

Customer service has evolved into a business strategy that helps companies differentiate themselves from their competition, sustain profitability and thrive in any type of economy, especially during recessionary times. It's often the only competitive advantage a business has.

Improving the customer experience has become a major strategic priority for just about every company, according to a report by Forrester Research, The State of the Customer Experience, 2012. Of all the businesses surveyed, 93% identified the customer experience among their strategic priorities, and

28% placed it at the top of the list. Additionally, 75% plan to use it as a key differentiator. Will you?

Even though many companies seem to have good intentions and plan to implement a customer-centric business strategy, customers continue to have poor service experiences. Sadly, according to the latest American Express Global Customer Service Barometer survey, 78% of customers have bailed somewhere in the buying process because of poor customer service.

Is Your Company Customer-Centric?

Think about your last few customer service experiences and rate how many were exceptional. Now think about how your customers might rate *their* experiences with your company. Are you following through on your good intentions to implement a customer-centric business strategy? We hope so. If not, now is the time to begin. Your process doesn't have to be complicated. Our five principles, along with the strategies we outline throughout this book, will provide you with a practical and simple approach to create a customer-centric company.

If your organization isn't customer focused or doesn't invest the time and resources to hire and train employees on the delivery of exceptional customer service, the chances of earning your customers' loyalty are greatly reduced. It's not enough to create policies and procedures for your employees to follow; you must make sure all employees and managers know why and how to go above and beyond customers' expectations and ensure they do so consistently.

Most companies recognize the importance of good customer service and understand the financial benefits of providing exceptional experiences to their customers. They're also probably aware of the "Four Rs," the business drivers that are linked to attracting and retaining loyal customers:

- Revenue—customers give your company a larger percentage of their wallet share, adding to your bottom line
- Retention— customers continue doing business with your company, reducing the cost of churn
- Referrals—customers refer their family members and friends to your company, allowing you to cost-effectively acquire new customers
- Reputation—customers speak well of your company, increasing public awareness, which attracts new customers and investors

Poor Customer Service: A Business Killer

It's not clear whether companies realize the potential cost of negative customer experiences. According to Parature's customer service blog, *"Poor customer experiences result in an estimated $83 billion loss by U.S. enterprises each year because of defections and abandoned purchases."* That's an alarming number and we don't want your company to contribute to it.

When customers have a bad experience with a company, they usually tell between 10 and 15 people about it, but often don't tell the company. That means the company doesn't have an opportunity to make it right and earn their loyalty. The Research Institute of America (RIA) states, *"An average business will never hear a word from 96% of their unhappy customers whose complaints range from poor service, rudeness, to discourteous treatment. These are the customers that silently move away from you and are welcomed with open-arms by the competition. These are the customers who tell their friends, co-workers, and family members about their bad experiences. Multiply the number of people these unhappy customers have told about their unsatisfactory experiences, and soon we realize that it's not just one customer leaving us — it's an army of lost customers and a pocketful of lost revenue."* This clearly shows that the negative financial effect of poor customer service is felt in two ways: the loss of an existing customer and the lost opportunity of a new customer.

When friends, family and colleagues ask for recommendations on companies to patronize, customers who've had bad experiences are the first to volunteer which companies **not** to use. Whether it's word-of-mouth or having negative comments posted on social media and review sites that can turn complaints into viral phenomena, you've got to make sure the stories your customers tell are positive.

If you don't know how your customers are feeling and what they're saying, your less-than-stellar customer service could slowly and silently kill your business. The Social Media for Customer Service Survey from ClickFox (2011) stated it this way: *"Word of mouth has a ripple effect on other customers. More than 60% of customers are influenced or very influenced by other customers' comments about companies."*

The Need for Employee Engagement

Your employees determine what kind of experiences your customers have with your company. No company can afford to have employees who are "renting" their jobs (as opposed to "owning" them), treating customers in a manner that conveys they just don't care. If your employees aren't engaged, your customers won't be either. To illustrate this, a study performed by Gallup and the federal government's General Services Administration (GSA) found that, *"workgroups with higher levels of engagement had, on average, 23% to 26% more highly satisfied and loyal customers, which equated to more than $1 million in revenue"* than workgroups with low or slightly engaged employees.

A well-known hospitality company provides another example that demonstrates the direct correlation between employee engagement and customer satisfaction. Through the efforts of Nigel Martin, former VP of Leadership and Learning at Harrah's Entertainment (now Caesar's Entertainment Inc.), the company embarked on a two-year initiative to improve internal employee engagement. At the conclusion of their efforts, Harrah's reported a customer satisfaction improvement of more than 10%.

What effect do disengaged employees have on your customers' experiences...and how much is that costing your company?

It's important to remember that customers aren't looking for transactions. They want relationships with you and your employees. They want personalization. They want to feel valued and appreciated by the companies with which they do business. How can you exceed their expectations? It's not rocket science. Make sure your company is staffed with engaged employees who take ownership of their jobs and care about providing consistent, memorable customer experiences.

While CEOs, business owners and managers emphasize the expectation of delighting customers, it's their employees who are most often responsible for delivering the experience. And, how you treat your employees will often influence how they treat your customers.

Here's an employee perspective on how much this matters: *"The customer service you receive at Brother's Trattoria is a direct reflection of the management team and the way they handle the serving team,"* said Megan Murphy, a server at this Beacon, New York restaurant. *"They're good to us, so we're good to the customers."*

Happy Employees Create Happy Customers

Adams Fairacre Farms, an establishment that's been around since 1919 and has expanded to four locations in New York's Hudson Valley, understands that correlation well. A key contributing factor to the company's long-term success is its devotion to quality service and genuine hospitality.

With a history of exceptional service, it's almost surprising that there's no formal training program in place. What's Adams Fairacre Farms' secret?

"There's nothing formal, so it's kind of unique," said Gaye Mallet, Director of Human Resources, *"but the owners are still involved and the managers have all been here long term. The customer service focus is passed down informally from the owners and managers, and it's effective, because people always say how they love the store. We always treat customers like family."*

Mallet continued, *"I think one of the things that contributes to good customer service is that the employees are happy here — they're treated fairly, they have great benefits, and we accommodate their schedules. If they aren't happy, they won't be friendly and engaging. Customers constantly tell us that people working here are so happy and that goes back to the owners. They treat the employees like extended family. Having worth and being happy helps deliver great customer service."*

Employees will model the behavior you demonstrate and pass that along to your customers, so never underestimate the influence you have on your team.

Meet Rant and Rave

Speaking of employees, it's time to introduce you to Rant and Rave, our two fictitious employees. As we mentioned in the introduction, Rant and Rave represent employees who may be working in your organization, taking care of your customers. If your employees are acting like Rant, they may:

- Only be working for a paycheck
- Not care whether customers are happy or not
- View customers as interruptions to their day
- Often be rude or impatient and have a negative tone
- Complain about the company and its leadership

- Tell customers what they can't do instead of what they can do

If your employees are acting like Rave, they will:

- Take ownership of their job and your customers
- Want to take care of customers
- Make customers feel special, giving them their undivided attention
- Smile and be pleasant and easy to deal with
- Do whatever it takes to make sure customers are happy
- Be advocates of the company

Are your employees acting more like Rant or more like Rave? Remember, how your employees act toward your customers will have a positive or negative effect on the experience they have with your company—and that will make a difference, positive or negative, on your bottom line.

Rant or Rave?

Think about the last time you had a bad customer service experience. Was the employee taking care of you acting more like Rant or more like Rave? How did the experience make you feel? Did you tell others about it? Would you do business with the company again?

Imagine if one of your customers had a similar bad customer service experience with your company and was ranting about it. While you might understand how this person feels, it's important to think about the consequences that sharing this bad experience with his friends, family, or colleagues can have on your business.

Here's a comment from a customer describing what it felt like when she was taken care of by an employee like Rant: "*I just want someone to 'own' me as a customer, whether things are going well or there's an issue. I called a service business to ask them to correct a problem. I was transferred to three different people, but the problem was never resolved. So, I called back and asked to speak with a manager. I was put on hold and no one ever came back to the phone. When I called a third time and explained my situation and what I needed, the person hung up on me. That's right. The person on the other end simply didn't want to talk to me or help resolve my issue. Can you imagine? Talk about lack of ownership. I'm done with them!*"

Could this be what some of your customers are saying when they deal with your company? What would the consequences be to your business?

Now imagine if one of your customers had a good experience with your company and was raving about it. How would you feel if that customer shared the good experience with her friends, family or colleagues and referred them to your business?

Let's hear how another customer felt when he was taken care of by an employee like Rave: *"I'm just back from a vacation and had an extraordinary experience in a restaurant. We walked in; they whisked us to our table, pushed chairs in as we sat down (every time, all night long!) and put the napkins in our laps. There were white napkins on the table, but if they saw someone with dark clothes, they immediately came over with a black napkin, taking away the white one. I also loved that several servers came out with the dishes, so as not to leave half the customers served and half not. Did I mention the food was excellent and I received a follow-up call to make sure we had a great experience?"*

We know you'd prefer this comment from your customers.

These customer comments provide a contrast between the positive and negative behaviors of employees like Rant and Rave. Are your employees behaving more like Rant or more like Rave? Think about the consequences to your business.

The Five Principles

Now that you've met Rant and Rave and we've illustrated the contrast between how they may be serving your customers, it's time to introduce our five principles:

1. Think Like An Owner

2. Build a Relationship

3. Remove the Roadblocks

4. Walk in Your Customer's Shoes

5. Capture Your Customer's Heart

We'll share the definitions and behaviors associated with each principle in the upcoming chapters. We believe these five principles are the building blocks to help you create a customer-centric business strategy that will lead to long-term customer relationships.

If you and your employees already act like Rave, congratulations. Use this book to complement what you're currently doing. If you're unsure whether you have employees like Rant or Rave or you know you need to improve your customers' experiences, this book will be invaluable to you.

Principle One: Think Like an Owner

"The moral of the story: perceptions are everything.

During each moment you are in contact with a

customer,

you are the organization."

Jan Carlzon, former CEO, SAS Group

Principle One: Think Like an Owner

"I DON'T KNOW. I DON'T WORK IN THIS DEPARTMENT."

Have you ever had a personal experience where you were taken care of by a company's owner? What kind of experience was it? We'll bet it was pretty good, maybe even exceptional— because most business owners know the way they treat their customers directly influences whether long-term relationships are established. They also know what effect *that* has on their bottom line. Very often, owners will go out of their way to make sure their customers are happy…and everyone who has an owner's mentality—regardless of their position in the company—will take care of customers as if they are the owner.

If everyone taking care of your customers thought like an owner, customers wouldn't have a reason to stop doing business with your company. Do *your* employees "think like an owner"? Do they treat customers the way you want them to? Do they make decisions that are in the best interest of the customer? Are they aware of how important each customer is to the long-term success of your business? Do they realize their future employment with your company is directly affected by how happy customers are with your service?

Employees Are Customers, Too

Employees often see themselves as just that, employees. They don't see themselves as "an owner" of the company. The good news is that you don't have to give your employees shares of company stock to inspire them to think like an owner. What you must do is treat them as well as you treat your customers.

Employees are your "internal" customers; how they're treated has a direct effect on how well they treat your "external" customers. When employees feel valued, trusted and respected and are empowered to make decisions, they're motivated to go out of their way to treat your customers well. When your customers are well cared for, they'll return and bring friends and family too.

If your customers don't have a good experience with your company, they won't come back. Additionally, there's a correlation between customer satisfaction and employee retention. If you start losing customers, you won't need or be able to retain all your employees.

If your employees don't think like an owner, they may be turning off your customers. What do we mean by think like an owner? Our definition is *to make decisions, solve problems and do what's right for customers as if you're the owner of the company.*

Obviously, the illustration at the beginning of this chapter doesn't depict Rant thinking like an owner. An owner would never tell a customer, "I don't know. I don't work in this department." An owner would help the customer, or at the very least, find someone who could.

Share Your Expectations

As CEOs, business owners and managers, it's your responsibility to educate your employees and provide them with examples of how you want your customers to be treated. Using specific examples is a good way to help employees understand what you mean and what you expect them to do. For example, you might review the following process you want them to follow to address customer complaints:

- Thank the customer for bringing the issue to their attention

- Apologize for the inconvenience the issue has caused

- Work to resolve the issue to the customer's satisfaction

By sharing examples of typical customer service scenarios and how you expect them to be handled, you'll exemplify what it means to think like an owner and what behaviors you expect your employees to demonstrate.

If you empower your employees to make decisions, solve problems and do what's right for the customer (whatever it takes), they'll begin to think and act like an owner of your company. As the owner, CEO, or manager, you aren't able to serve all your customers yourself, so having employees who think like an owner will ensure your customers are taken care of in the manner you'd treat them yourself.

What Would Rant Do?

What came to mind when you read this comic strip? Are you concerned that this might be how employees behave in your business?

There are specific behaviors associated with the *Think Like an Owner* principle. It's important to identify the ones you don't want your employees displaying with your customers.

The list of negative behaviors (actions Rant might take) will help raise your awareness and define your expectations with your employees.

Here are the behaviors and actions that might be displayed when an employee like Rant is taking care of customers:

- *Unnecessarily passing customers to another employee*
  Example: Referring customer to a co-worker rather than helping them
- *Not taking an interest in customers or their needs*
  Example: Ignoring customers when they need help
- *Trivializing customers' problems*
  Example: Telling customers, "I can't believe you're making a big deal about this"
- *Making customers feel like they're an interruption*
  Example: Rolling eyes and asking "Yes?" when customers approach them while they're speaking with another employee

Later in this chapter, we'll contrast these behaviors with those an employee like Rave might display with customers.

The Cost of Bad Customer Service

As you can imagine, not having employees who think like owners can quickly turn off customers, but it does much more than that; it negatively affects your revenue and customer retention. There are extensive research findings that support the direct correlation between employees doing the bare minimum and what that may cost a company.

According to The Wharton School's David Sirota and Louis Mischkind, who based their findings on 30 years of research involving 2.5 million employees in 237 companies, organizations with high morale outperform their competitors by roughly 20%. In contrast, companies whose employees are discouraged and do just enough to get by suffer when it comes to results. What's the cost of bad service to your company?

When it comes to retention and reputation, according to the White House Office of Consumer Affairs, happy customers who get their issue resolved tell about four to six people about their experience. If your employees understand that—and realize the potential result of their behaviors—they're more likely to perform the actions and display the behaviors you expect…and your customers deserve.

Time for Reflection

Take time to think about your actions, and those of your employees, and answer the question below.

What behaviors are your employees demonstrating related to the *Think Like an Owner* principle that could be negatively affecting your Four Rs (revenue, retention, referrals and reputation)?

_____

_____

_____

_____

_____

_____

It's Not About the Shoes

You might be surprised at how many opportunities there are to differentiate your company through customer service. Tony Hseih is the CEO of Zappos, a company that primarily sells shoes…but may be just as well known for being all about the customer experience. Here's a true story, in Tony's words, to illustrate just what we mean:

"I'm reminded of a time when I was in Santa Monica, California a few years ago at a Skechers sales conference. After a long night of barhopping, a small group of us headed up to someone's hotel room to order some food. My friend from Skechers tried to order a pepperoni pizza from the room service menu, but was disappointed to learn that the hotel we were staying at did not deliver hot food after 11 p.m. We had missed the deadline by several hours.

A few of us cajoled her into calling Zappos to try to order a pizza. She took us up on our dare, turned on the speakerphone, and explained to the (very) patient Zappos rep that she was staying in a Santa Monica hotel and really craving a pepperoni pizza, that room service was no longer delivering hot food, and that she wanted to know if there was anything Zappos could do to help.

The Zappos rep was initially a bit confused by the request, but she quickly recovered and put us on hold. She returned two minutes later, listing the five closest places in the Santa Monica area that were still open and delivering pizzas."

This story is a good example of a customer-centric business strategy. Imagine if all your employees were responding to customers in this manner; it would be like having a whole company of employees like Rave serving your customers.

What Would Rave Do?

Clearly, Rave's behaviors—which reflect thinking like an owner—contrast drastically with Rant's. The benefits of your employees thinking like an owner positively influence your company's reputation and future referrals, both of which have a direct effect on your revenue. Remember, happy customers who get their issue resolved tell about four to six people about their experience.

Here are the behaviors and actions that might be displayed when an employee like Rave is taking care of customers:

- *Taking responsibility for customers even if it's not your job*
  Example: Processing a credit rather than transferring customers to the accounting department to have them do it

- *Doing whatever it takes to make sure customers are satisfied*
  Example: Answering customers' questions and confirming their needs were met

- *Making customers your top priority*
  Example: Giving customers your undivided attention

- *Resolving customers' problems even if you didn't cause them*
  Example: Telling customers, "I can take care of that for you"

An Employee's Perspective

What does an employee who displays these behaviors think about customer service and specifically this principle? The following insight from waitress Julia Machover is something to share with your employees, as they may be able to relate to her.

Julia is a waitress while she's pursuing a business degree, but she takes her role seriously; it's much more to her than just earning some extra cash. Julia values her job at Seasons 52 restaurant in Garden City, New York and firmly believes in going the extra mile.

"I've been working as a server since I was 16, so it's really the only job I've ever known," Julia said, *"but through my experience, my number one priority is ensuring guests have the best experience possible. It's taken me a while to get to that point because at first it was just a job; I was doing it because I needed the money, because I was forced to, or whatever the case may be. Now, working in hospitality for so long, I've realized that when I go out to a restaurant and eat as a guest, I notice so many things that can make or break my experience. I try to treat guests how I'd want to be treated if I was sitting in the booth."*

Julia finds that a lot of customers who frequent the restaurant ask for her as their server. Having had the pleasure of being served by her, we're not surprised. Julia is told customers' names before she's even made her way to their table. This way, customers can be addressed by their names to create a more personalized experience.

Julia explained that she strives to stay one step ahead of her guests in order to offer them a memorable experience. Whether it's filling a glass with more water or offering extra napkins, she's constantly thinking of things she can do for her guests before they ask. Julia advised us that she's *"not trying to do the bare minimum, but trying to improve the overall."*

Given her wisdom about the value of customers, we weren't surprised that Julia had a wonderful response when asked about our principles. *"Think Like an Owner really stood out to me. Customers come in and they want to sit down and relax. I'm the one who's responsible for them and in the end, I want them to come back."*

Julia's comments provide an honest perspective and powerful example of how an employee who thinks like an owner can positively affect a company's Four Rs.

Rant or Rave

You know that employees like Rant don't think like owners. The Zappos employee and the waitress at Seasons 52 restaurant model Rave's actions and behaviors. It is obvious that these employees understand this principle. In fact when you think about the Zappos employee and the fact that they don't even sell pizza, she demonstrated extraordinary effort and ownership that helped the customer satisfy their need.

What would your employees do in a similar situation? Would they think like the employee at Zappos? Do your employees think like Julia and take responsibility for their customer's experience?

These two employees truly demonstrate the value of having employees who act like Rave and think like owners.

Time for Reflection

Take a few minutes to think about your actions, and those of your employees, and answer the questions below.

What behaviors are your employees demonstrating related to the *Think Like an Owner* principle that could positively affect your Four Rs (revenue, retention, referrals and reputation)?

_____

_____

_____

_____

_____

_____

When you think about the behaviors you and your employees are currently displaying toward your customers with regard to thinking like an owner, are they more like Rant's or more like Rave's?

_____

_____

_____

_____

_____

_____

View From the Top

You've heard from an employee about the importance of thinking like an owner. Now let's hear from a business owner.

Scrubadoo is a fairly new company that's rapidly expanding. Their products include medical scrubs and nursing uniforms. The success that's led to this growth is strongly attributed to the high regard with which customers are held.

"Do what's right," said Brett Bohl, Scrubadoo's owner. *"When I bring on new employees, I tell them, 'You have the power to do what's right.' If there is ever an issue and the right thing to do is refund the customer and still deliver their product anyway, you can make that decision. The customer always comes first."*

Brett makes sure he and his staff are on top of their customers' needs, and most importantly, living up to their customers' expectations. Scrubadoo makes it a point to ensure that not a single customer is neglected or ignored. *"As far as our policy,"* Brett explained, *"it's be upfront. Get back to people in a timely manner, set expectations and follow through with them."*

Each and every customer at Scrubadoo is treated with undivided attention, and an extreme amount of hospitality. As soon as orders are placed, customers are advised when they'll ship. Once orders have shipped, customers are contacted again, informed when they'll be delivered, and given the name and contact information of an employee who'll serve as their direct contact in the event anything goes wrong. When Scrubadoo orders are fulfilled, customers receive handwritten letters of appreciation for their business. Oftentimes, a 10% off or "free shipping on your next order" coupon is enclosed.

In addition to clearly going the extra mile, Brett is a firm believer in offering his employees ownership over their positions. Aside from his coaching, role-playing occurs and new employees receive handbooks containing the basic customer service principles Scrubadoo follows.

"I think you should try to get your employees to buy into thinking like an owner. That's a great principle," Brett said. *"One way to do that is empowerment. My employees know they have the ability to do things like refunding the customer or sending someone a $25 gift certificate; they don't have to ask me for permission. They have the answer right away and it makes them feel better about their jobs. They don't have to tell the customer, 'Let me check with…' They have ownership over their positions."*

Right from their job interview, potential employees are aware of what the Scrubadoo team is passionate about: customer service and satisfaction. Team members are offered freedom and encouragement. *"Customer relationships are important,"* Brett noted. *"We put a lot of time, effort and money into them. There's no incentive program for providing good customer service; that's the core of our business. If you don't do it, you're not going to work here."*

When you look at Brett's comments in combination with Julia's, it's easy to see how the *Think Like an Owner* principle can be applied and the obvious impact it has on actual customer experiences. As you think about how you can apply this principle in your company, to ensure you have a team of employees who act like Rave, we've provided some strategies to assist you.

Think Like an Owner Action Strategies

- Define what it means to you to serve customers and communicate that to your employees.

- Help your employees develop strong decision-making skills.

- Communicate what you expect your employees to do to serve customers in your absence.

- Establish what it means to go above and beyond customers' expectations.

- Coach your employees for success. Give immediate feedback when they demonstrate an action or behavior that contributes to thinking like an owner.

Call to Action

What action steps can I take to bring this principle to life in my company?

1. _____

   _____

   _____

   _____

   _____

2. _____

   _____

   _____

   _____

   _____

3. _____

   _____

   _____

   _____

   _____

Principle Two: Build a Relationship

"People don't care how much you know

until they know how much you care."

John C. Maxwell, Author

Developing the Leader Within You

Principle Two: Build a Relationship

First impressions make or break opportunities to build relationships. Customers' first impressions of a company often determine whether or not they'll ever return. First impressions create perceptions—of companies and employees—that can leave customers feeling good, bad or indifferent. If employees don't make positive connections each and every time they interact with customers, the company may be losing the opportunity to build long-term relationships.

Have you ever called a company and decided not to do business with it because you felt the employee with whom you spoke had no interest in serving you? Or perhaps you walked into a store, couldn't find anyone to help you or felt the person who was attempting to help you really didn't seem like she wanted to and you walked out? These examples demonstrate the importance of first impressions—they influence customers' buying decisions and can negatively affect companies' opportunities to build relationships.

What do we mean by build a relationship? Our definition is *to establish rapport, demonstrate you care, and show genuine interest in your customers and their needs.*

Obviously, the illustration at the beginning of this chapter doesn't depict employees establishing rapport and taking a genuine interest in the customer—yet establishing rapport is a vital step to gaining customer trust and it sets the tone for the entire interaction.

You Had Me at Hello

Setting a positive tone by acknowledging and greeting customers is critical to establishing rapport. Next, it's important for employees to show they care by taking a genuine interest in customers' needs. This means employees are engaged with customers, which will often lead to positive experiences. Unfortunately, this rapport building doesn't typically happen, which can cause customers to lose interest and companies to lose business. The tone of a customer interaction is usually set in the first 10 seconds; that's how fast impressions can be formed and customers decide how they feel about a particular employee…and by association, the company. If customers aren't feeling good about the employees serving them, it gives them a reason to rant and take their business elsewhere.

The importance of this particular principle is the fact that if you don't practice it, you risk losing the opportunity to establish and maintain long-term relationships and earn customers' loyalty. The cost is enormous; this principle has a direct effect on your Four Rs.

According to TARP, the world's premier customer experience agency, customer churn is caused by feelings of poor treatment 68% of the time. These feelings begin with customers' first impressions and may or may not continue throughout entire interactions. Regardless, if two of every three customers feel they're being treated poorly, that makes it impossible to build long-term relationships with them. What's the bottom line? Customer churn is expensive.

Focus on the Entire Experience

While customer perception of the employee interactions they have with your company is a major component of first impressions, it isn't the only one. The physical appearance of your business (interior and exterior) also has a lot to do with how customers perceive your company. Remember, it's the entire experience that generates the feelings customers have when they do business with your company.

Through observation and many service audits, we've found that if companies consistently practiced just this one principle, *Build a Relationship,* the statistic cited by TARP could be reduced dramatically and they'd have a "standalone" competitive advantage.

According to RightNow Technologies Customer Experience Impact Report 2011, 50% of customers will give you one week to respond to a question before they stop doing business with you. This illustrates the value of demonstrating you care and showing genuine interest in your customers and their needs. It also reminds us of the negative financial consequences of losing customers.

What Would Rant Do?

What came to mind when you read this comic strip? Are you concerned that this may be how employees behave in your business?

There are specific behaviors associated with the *Build a Relationship* principle. It's important to identify the ones you don't want your employees displaying with your customers.

The list of negative behaviors (actions Rant might take) will help raise your awareness and define your expectations with your employees.

Here are the behaviors and actions that might be displayed when an employee like Rant is taking care of customers:

- *Displaying negative body language*

  Example: Not maintaining eye contact or smiling when speaking with customers

- *Not greeting customers*

  Example: Saying "Next" versus "Good morning, how may I help you"?

- *Pushing products rather than asking questions to uncover customer needs*

  Example: Assuming they know what customers want without asking them

- *Acting disinterested in customers*

  Example: Not listening to customers and being

distracted by other employees, their cell phone or
something else

Later in this chapter, we'll contrast these behaviors with
those an employee like Rave might display with customers.

Reality Check: FedEx

A hilariously sad video of a FedEx deliveryman chucking a
computer monitor attracted nearly 200,000 views on YouTube
in a single day. Many of those people expressed fears that their
packages would be treated with the same disregard. The 21-
second clip shows the deliveryman taking the package from the
back of a FedEx-branded van parked outside a home. He then
walks alongside an iron gate enclosing the residence and past
what appears to be a security keypad that might buzz him in.
Without missing a beat, its fragile contents are tossed onto a
driveway on the other side of the gate.

The deliveryman marches back to the van without any
regard for the customer or his merchandise. The saddest part of
this story is that the customer was home at the time, with the
front door wide open. All the deliveryman would have had to
do was ring the bell on the gate to safely give the package to the
customer. Even though this is an egregious example of
customer service, it illustrates the lack of caring and interest in
customer needs.

Time for Reflection

Take time to think about your actions, and those of your employees, and answer the question below.

What behaviors are your employees demonstrating related to the *Build a Relationship* principle that could be negatively affecting your Four Rs (revenue, retention, referrals and reputation)?

_____

_____

_____

_____

_____

_____

Your Customers Have Names; Use Them

When was the last time a customer service representative used *your* name during a conversation? How did it make you feel? This is a fundamental aspect of establishing rapport. People love to hear their names; it personalizes the interaction and shows genuine interest in them.

Sadly, "employees only ask for the customer's name 21% of the time (the person has a name 100% of the time)" according to ContactPoint Client Research. This is really unfortunate, since this is one of the easiest actions that contribute to providing quality customer service.

Coach your employees that when they don't know customers' names, they can ask for them; this is a way to establish rapport and build relationships. There are also other ways for employees to learn customers' names, such as making note of them from information they already have, or reading them from a customer's credit card, personal check or driver's license.

Don't Forget Follow-up

Every time customers do business with your company, they form an impression, and what you do before, during, and after they leave or hang up the phone will ultimately determine if you're able to build long-term relationships. Notice that we included "after" behavior, i.e., follow-up, which demonstrates the value of the relationship, builds trust, and most importantly, shows customers you appreciate them doing business with you. Follow-up can be purpose-driven, to learn more about customers' future needs, or it can be a simple thank-you note or call.

The process you put in place can vary in sophistication based on the size of your company and how often you want to follow up with your customers. Client Relationship Management (CRM) solutions ranging from simple to complex software programs are readily available. The most important action you must take is establishing an expectation within your organization to thank your customers and follow up with them. Your follow-up method is less important than making a commitment to doing it. It's a critical step toward building relationships.

What Would Rave Do?

Clearly, Rave's behavior—which reflects a focus on building a relationship—contrasts drastically from Rant's. Just think about the dramatic reduction in customer churn and the increased opportunities to build relationships that come from practicing these behaviors. How are your employees establishing rapport and demonstrating genuine interest in your customers' needs?

Here are the behaviors and actions that might be displayed when an employee like Rave is taking care of customers:

- *Establishing rapport by acknowledging customers*
  Example: Asking for and using customers' names during conversations

- *Remembering customers*
  Example: Asking repeat customers about something they shared with you the last time you spoke to them

- *Thanking customers for their business*
  Example: Telling customers you appreciate them doing business with your company

- *Following up with customers*
  Example: Telling customers you'll call them back and then doing so

An Employee's Perspective

What does an actual employee who displays these behaviors think about customer service and specifically this principle? The following insight from service advisor Peter Leonardi is something to share with your employees, as they may be able to relate to him.

"My personal philosophy on service, I'd say, is to always try and find out what your customer wants. They're there for a reason and you have to kind of decode what they say and what they're doing and convert that into what they want, you know, what's going to make them happy," Peter said. *"It's connecting the problem to the solution.*

When it gets down to it, I just like to fix people's problems, I like to fix things and if you're having an issue with something that I have control over, that I can get fixed, I want to connect you to that answer," he continued. *"I want to make sure you're happy and you keep coming back. I just want to do right by people and make it right for them."*

Peter is flattered that his customers at Healey Brothers in Beacon, New York continue to ask for him. Understanding the value of relationship building, he took his passion for exceptional customer service and started to think outside the box. Without being asked to do so, he started sending thank-you cards to his loyal customers.

"You always have to connect with people; that's the most important thing," Peter noted. *"Whatever it is that you do, you have to connect with what you're doing and who you're doing it with. You have to bring people in and take care of them like you would want to get taken care of. If you're not thinking like an owner, try to at least think like a consumer."*

Peter isn't only recognized by his customers; he's recognized by his colleagues, and more importantly, his general manager. With that said, we were curious to hear if Peter had any advice to give to those in customer service positions. He offered this response:

"I'd say to anyone in any position, don't get mad at your money. You're there getting paid to do this job. When someone comes in angry, or somebody gives you a job and it's hot outside and you don't feel like working on it, or someone has you get a part and you don't want to get it—don't get frustrated. That's why you're there, that's why you're getting paid, that's what you're there to do."

Rant or Rave?

The thoughts Peter shared show he understands how important it is to connect with his customers. Compare Peter's personal philosophy and his desire to make customers happy to the FedEx deliveryman's—there's a stark contrast. What is your employees' philosophy on service? If it's not in alignment with your expectations, start a dialogue with them and seize the opportunity to have a "teachable moment."

Time for Reflection

Take a few minutes to think about your actions, and those of your employees, and answer the questions below.

What behaviors are your employees practicing related to the *Build a Relationship* principle that could positively affect your Four Rs (revenue, retention, referrals and reputation)?

_____

_____

_____

_____

_____

_____

When you think about the behaviors you and your employees are currently displaying toward your customers with regard to building relationships, are they more like Rant's or more like Rave's?

_____

_____

_____

_____

_____

_____

_____

View From the Top

You've heard from an employee about the importance of building a relationship. Now let's hear from a CEO.

"We recognize that the only sustainable competitive advantage is the quality of our people and the service we provide," said Ronald Bentley, CEO of Chemung Canal Trust Company in Elmira, New York. *"I'm proud to say that we have made client service a competitive differentiator for Chemung Canal."*

The Chemung Canal Trust Company calls quality customer service "CanalCare," this service promise is extended to both external and internal clients. It's understood that the quality of their service is what sets them apart and gives them a "distinct competitive advantage."

Like all quality customer service, the operation begins with the staff. *"There are only two jobs in our company: those that serve our external clients and those that serve those who are serving our clients,"* explained Bentley. *"Phone calls will be returned in no more than one business day. If a client needs to meet after hours or on weekends, we'll arrange it. Whenever possible, customer service will be delivered face-to-face. Staff will take ownership and do everything possible to help solve a problem or meet a need. We're always eager to offer additional assistance. Clients can expect a one-hour consumer loan turnaround following a loan appointment."*

Bentley believes in the importance of customer feedback. Every few years, a client satisfaction survey is administered, and he strives for the results to be no less than "great."

"Employees are empowered to do what it takes to fix a problem and turn an unhappy client into a loyal ambassador for Chemung Canal," Bentley said.

When you look at Bentley's comments in combination with Peter's, it's easy to see how the *Build a Relationship* principle can be applied and the obvious effect it has on actual customer experiences. As you think about how you can apply this principle in your company, to ensure you have a team of employees who act like Rave, we've provided some strategies to assist you.

Build a Relationship Action Strategies

- Implement a service interaction model that includes building rapport.

- Strive to use customers' names 100% of the time.

- Establish a practice within in your organization to follow up with your customers.

- Thank your customers each and every time they do business with your company.

- Coach your employees for success. Give immediate feedback when they demonstrate an action or behavior that contributes to building a relationship.

Call to Action

What action steps can I take to bring this principle to life in my company?

1. _____

   _____

   _____

   _____

   _____

2. _____

   _____

   _____

   _____

   _____

3. _____

   _____

   _____

   _____

   _____

~ 1 ~
Think Like An Owner
~ 2 ~
Build a Relationship

Principle Three: Remove the Roadblocks

"The biggest reason that positive endings don't happen is because employees are trained on policies and rules rather than principles."

Jeffrey Gitomer, author,
Customer Satisfaction is Worthless,
Customer Loyalty is Priceless

Principle Three: Remove the Roadblocks

Customers want to patronize companies that make it easy to do business with them. Your customers have many choices when it comes to deciding which company to use. If you don't make it easy for them to access your products or services, they'll find a company that will.

According to the Corporate Executive Board Study, there's an 86% likelihood that customers will purchase products from companies that simplify the purchase journey. Wouldn't you like to increase your odds of customers doing business with you by making it easy for them to do so? You realize that customers who purchase from you and have a good experience will in all probability refer others to your business.

At Ritz-Carlton hotels, each staff member is authorized to spend up to $2,000 per guest per day to resolve customer complaints. According to Sharmon Walters, Manager of Southwest's People Department, Southwest Airlines employees are empowered to make decisions that provide outrageous customer service, even if it's coloring outside the line of what's normally done. Nordstrom once refunded the purchase of a set of tires despite the fact that the store has never sold tires. These are a few examples of removing the roadblocks from a customer's experience. Your company doesn't have to be one of the larger, well-known brands to make it easy for customers to do business with you.

What do we mean by remove the roadblocks? Our definition is to *eliminate obstacles that get in the customer's way of doing business with you.*

The illustration at the beginning of the chapter depicts a situation in which the customer is unable to do business with the company because the employee (Rant) isn't making it easy for him to find what he needs. Can you imagine your employees not helping a customer who very well could be their grandfather! Imagine if all your employees treated every customer the way they'd want *their* grandfather treated, especially when it relates to the *Remove the Roadblocks* principle?

We go out of our way to take care of people who are important to us. Aren't your customers important to you and your business? Of course they are—which is why it's critical to eliminate anything that can get in their way of being served by you (and sending them to the competition).

Are Your Policies Customer-Friendly?

If your policies aren't customer-friendly, if you ask your customers to do the work you should be doing on their behalf, or if you make customers jump through hoops, the message you're sending is that you're less concerned about customers and more concerned about making it easy for you and your company.

Nordstrom is a good example of practicing customer-friendly policies; its employee policy manual is only two sentences long: *"Use good judgment in all situations. There will be no additional rules."* Nordstrom is well known for its high-quality customer service and doing whatever it takes to make it easy to do business at its stores.

Another company known for its exceptional service is Stew Leonard's, a food and dairy store named one of Fortune 100's Best Companies to Work ten years in a row. Its service policy, "Service Rock of Commitment," consists of two rules:

- Rule #1: The customer is always right!
- Rule #2: If the customer is ever wrong, read rule #1.

These rules are displayed on a slab of granite outside each of Stew Leonard's five stores. All employees know they can do anything in their power to make customers happy.

What can you glean from Nordstrom's and Stew Leonard's service policies? You can have guidelines that are simple and short when employees are trained on how to treat their customers.

Customers can't be loyal to your company if you make it difficult for them to do business with you. If you don't remove the roadblocks, your customers won't think twice about looking for a company that will. And let's not forget that loyal customers are one of your company's most valuable assets.

While removing the roadblocks may sometimes reduce a company's revenue in the short term, by way of a refund or adjustment, the goal is that you'll make up any deficit in the long run by creating loyal customers. Losing a customer is far more expensive than losing money on a particular transaction.

Don't "Phone It In"

Prompt responses to customer concerns, empowering employees to make decisions in the absence of a manager, and being accessible to answer questions are some of the ways customer-centric companies remove the roadblocks to doing business with them. For instance, when calling a company, most customers prefer being greeted by a live person rather than an impersonal automated attendant.

According to a recent Reuter's survey in *Consumer Reports*, the top three reasons causing telephone customer angst are not getting a human on the phone, too many phone steps, and a long wait on hold. If a phone rings five or six times before it's answered, or if customers have to go through prompt after prompt just to get routed to someone who can finally help them, you're at a disadvantage by the time they reach a company representative. Have you called into your company to determine whether you're putting roadblocks in front of your customers?

Be Proactive and Flexible

It's not a complex process to eliminate roadblocks. For instance, customers don't like when their orders are delayed, but if you let them know about the situation before they call to inquire about shipment status, you can often prevent unpleasant fallout. Problems and complaints are a part of doing business, but if you're responsive to customers, or even better, proactive, you have the chance to turn possible negatives into opportunities to build customer loyalty.

Exercising flexibility with customers means just what it sounds like; you should be able to bend in many ways, if necessary. Rigid policies or procedures can be roadblocks. Sometimes, we get set in our policies and procedures and we lose the flexibility we need to maintain our relationships with customers.

What Would Rant Do?

What came to mind when you read this comic strip? Are you concerned that this may be how employees behave in your business?

There are specific behaviors associated with the *Remove the Roadblocks* principle. It's important to identify the ones you don't want your employees displaying with your customers.

The list of negative behaviors (actions Rant might take) will help raise your awareness and define your expectations with your employees.

Here are the behaviors and actions that might be displayed when an employee like Rant is taking care of customers:

- *Not demonstrating flexibility*

  Example: Telling a customer, "I can't help you. This is the company's policy."

- *Not demonstrating a willingness to help*

  Example: Not offering to help customers when the person they ask for isn't available

- *Asking for information that's already been provided*

  Example: Asking for customers' account numbers after they've been entered into your automated system

- *Not proactively communicating relevant information*

  Example: Not informing customers about pricing changes that affect them

Later in this chapter, we'll contrast these behaviors with those an employee like Rave might display with customers.

Reality Check: America Online

You may be familiar with the story we're about to share with you. The effect of this particular customer experience in 2006 changed the company forever and continues to be relevant today. America Online found out how scripted customer service representatives can sound when a New York man recorded his attempt to cancel his service.

After hearing numerous horror stories about how hard it was to cancel an AOL account, Vincent Ferrari decided to tape his attempt at turning off his account. What ensued was a lengthy call that included Vincent's constant, yet polite pleas for the customer service representative to process the cancellation.

Rather than yield to Vincent's request, the AOL representative kept reading from a script, asking questions about how much Vincent used the account and what kind of Internet connection he had—and eventually asking to speak with the 30-year-old's father.

At one point, Vincent said, *"When I say, 'Cancel the account,' I don't mean, 'Figure out how to help me keep it.' I mean, 'Cancel the account.'"*

The call lasted 21 minutes, but its aftermath was far lengthier for AOL.

Vincent posted a video of the recorded call on his blog and it immediately went viral, landing him on the "Today Show" and in the *New York Times* and prompting AOL to publicly apologize.

"We have zero tolerance for customer-care incidents like this—which is deeply regrettable and also absolutely inexcusable," an AOL spokesman said, adding that the customer service representative was fired for his actions.

Cautionary tale about using scripts—don't use them.

The Customer Has Spoken

Unfortunately, what Vincent experienced wasn't a one-time occurrence; many customers have had experiences like his with various companies. Here are actual customers' comments about roadblocks they've experienced:

- "Why do I have to explain my problem again? I just told the person I was talking to all about it."
- "Why do representatives ask me for my account number when I just keyed it into the phone?"
- "Why can't you just issue me a credit? Why do I have to speak to a supervisor?"
- "Why should I have to prove that the item is on sale? It should be in the computer."
- "I don't want to call back later when that person comes back from lunch. Why can't you take a message and ask her to call me back?"
- "I called ahead of time and placed my order, so why wasn't it ready when I came to pick it up?"
- "Why should I have to go online to update my account when I'm on the phone with you and you have access to my account?"

What roadblocks are you putting up for your customers?

Time for Reflection

Take time to think about your actions, and those of your employees, and answer the question below.

What behaviors are your employees displaying related to the *Remove the Roadblocks* principle that could be negatively affecting your Four Rs (revenue, retention, referrals and reputation)?

_____

_____

_____

_____

_____

_____

The Magic of Exceptional Service

Another famed story is of the Portland, Oregon man who needed an Armani tuxedo for his daughter's wedding. As a last-ditch effort to find the tuxedo, he went to the local Nordstrom. His personal shopper took his measurements and asked for a little time to work on it.

The customer left and the next day he received a phone call from Nordstrom saying it had found the tux and it would be ready the following day. That day, he drove to Nordstrom, tried on the tux and found it fit perfectly. Nordstrom had altered the tux for free. He asked his Nordstrom personal shopper how she did it. She just smiled, shrugged and said, "Magic."

He wanted a more specific answer, so the Nordstrom personal shopper explained that after he left the store, she'd immediately worked to solve the problem by utilizing her connections and finding the tux on the other side of the continent in New York. The New York distributor immediately put the tux on a truck bound for Chicago, and a Chicago Nordstrom employee retrieved it at a rest stop. The Chicago Nordstrom over-nighted the tux to Portland and altered it to fit perfectly.

This story reflects incredible service, but it has an even more unbelievable twist: Nordstrom doesn't even sell Armani tuxedos.

What Would Rave Do?

Clearly, Rave's behavior—which reflects a focus on removing the roadblocks—contrasts drastically from Rant's. Rave recognizes that the customer is frustrated and apologizes for the difficulty she's been experiencing. Are your employees looking for opportunities to make it easy for your customers to do business with you?

Here are the behaviors and actions that might be displayed when an employee like Rave is taking care of customers:

- *Making it easy for customers*

  Example: Offering to look up information for customers rather than having them do it themselves

- *Demonstrating a sense of empowerment*

  Example: Making a decision you think your manager would make if he was faced with a similar situation

- *Telling customers what you can do*

  Example: Offering customers another option rather than telling them, "No, I can't"

- *Anticipating potential problems and taking steps to resolve them before they affect customers*

  Example: Proactively communicating a product is on backorder so customers can plan accordingly

An Employee's Perspective

Consider sharing the following perspective with your employees, as it demonstrates how effortless it can be to remove the roadblocks.

Luann Daniels isn't only a bookkeeper at the Chalfonte Hotel in Cape May, New Jersey; she also takes reservations and is in charge of the front desk staff.

"I remind them that they're the face of the hotel, they represent the hotel to the customer," said Luann, who believes in a good relationship with her staff. *"I empower them to make decisions. 'I have to ask the manager' gets really old. For example, if someone says they were unhappy with their dinner, I let them make a decision like giving them credit for tomorrow night's dinner. They [the customer]*

get an apology and a solution right away, rather than having to wait while a manager is tracked down and then needing to explain the whole story again."

Luann believes that the customer service representatives are usually lowest on the totem pole. For someone earning minimum wage, a difficult, angry customer can be a lot to deal with.

"*I think it really matters how the management above them treats and supports them,*" Luann said. "*They need support, they need sympathy and they need someone to tell them when they made a good decision.*"

Throughout her employment at the Chalfonte Hotel, and in other positions she's held, Luann has believed in building relationships with her customers.

"*I like to know who these people are,*" she explained. "*It also makes them feel connected and that they belong.*"

Luann is genuinely interested in her customers and she knows that something as simple as remembering a customer's name can go a long way. With a warm gesture like that, Luann finds customers stop at the front desk simply just to say 'hi,' which make her feel like she's making a difference.

"*Be helpful,*" Luann declared. "*I also try not to be formal. I just want to get done what the customer is asking for. I think about how I would feel on the receiving end of a call. I want to hear a friendly voice. Sometimes people get so formal that they're not friendly. I think talking to a pleasant person matters."*

Luann is a firm believer that a positive customer experience lays within the Golden Rule. She's fair and is aware that when customers are unreasonable, it's often due to a miscommunication. When those arise, Luann tries her hardest to satisfy her customers. She asks what they expected that they didn't receive. If it isn't an error on the hotel's part, Luann takes another step to ask what would make each particular customer happy. It's all about the way the situation is handled.

"Attitude is a choice," Luann affirmed. *"You can say, 'I have to talk to this grouchy lady' or you can try to win this lady over. Sometimes if you turn it around, it becomes a conversation and most of the time at the end of the conversation, a customer is satisfied. Everybody you talk to you have to treat as your advertising."*

Rant or Rave?

Luann's story illustrates how she's empowered and how she empowers others to do whatever it takes so customers get what they want. This kind of behavior leads to customers wanting to do business with your company, and that has a positive effect on your Four Rs. When you compare Luann's behavior to the behavior of the AOL employee who put roadblocks in front of the customer, you can see the obvious negative impact to the customer and to the company's reputation.

Eliminate Policy Roadblocks

A study by Maritz Research found that employees often feel their hands are tied by corporate policies that focus on bottom-line needs rather than those of the customers they're supposed to serve. Only 8% of the employees surveyed say their company's policies and procedures make it easy to satisfy customers, while just 13% have the authority needed to respond promptly to customer problems and requests.

Do you need to review your policies and procedures to see if they're putting up roadblocks for your customers? Are they preventing your employees from making it easy to satisfy your customers? If you answered "yes" to either of those questions, this would be a good time to consider making changes — to ensure your customers don't defect to companies that make it easy to do business with them.

Time for Reflection

Take a few minutes to think about your actions, and those of your employees, and answer the questions below.

What behaviors are your employees practicing related to the *Remove the Roadblocks* principle that could positively affect your Four Rs (revenue, retention, referrals and reputation)?

_____

_____

_____

_____

_____

_____

When you think about the behaviors you and your employees are currently displaying toward your customers when it comes to removing the roadblocks, are they more like Rant's or more like Rave's?

_____

_____

_____

_____

_____

_____

View from the Top

"I guess it's kind of cliché, but the customer's always right," stated Ken MacDonald, owner of MacDonald Marine in Mahopac, New York. *"Whatever the customer's need is, we try and take care of it."*

MacDonald Marine has been family owned and operated since the very first day it opened its doors, more than 50 years ago. The company's devotion to customer service has earned it loyalty, but most importantly, long-term customers.

"It's the little things," said MacDonald. *"If you're a new boater and you're a little bit tentative or apprehensive about getting in the boat and driving around, we'll get in, show you how everything works, help you tie up for the first time, and talk to you about the little things you need to know. It's not like 'Here you go, here's your boat,' and take off."*

MacDonald Marine has never really offered formal customer service training to its staff, but provides informal coaching about the way the establishment wishes to treat its customers. New employees are advised to be friendly and helpful, and greet customers upon entrance into the marina. Motivation, believes MacDonald, lies within his relationship with his employees. He often rewards his staff for exceptional service through bonuses.

"It's really an attitude type of thing," advised MacDonald. *"I try to gauge employees on what they can and cannot do."*

Still, MacDonald is convinced that excellent customer service is beyond just being friendly and helpful. Each year, a "Dockers Barbeque" is held, during which MacDonald cooks hotdogs and hamburgers to all those who dock at his marina. Customers are even recognized for their devotion; one received a personalized plaque for his 50th year of commitment to the company.

"If we're on more of a friendly basis with customers, they're more apt to talk to you and tell you where you've failed," MacDonald said.

MacDonald insists on trying to get to know his customers and is a firm believer in establishing relationships with them, whether they're looking to dock their boats or walking in to buy parts. Talking to people about themselves unlocks a different dimension of emotions, which starts to build rapport and a relationship.

"My name is on the front of the building, you know?" MacDonald pointed out. *"When someone is upset, it really hits home. You feel like you've let them down on more than one level."*

When you look at MacDonald's comments in combination with Luann's, it's easy to see how the *Remove the Roadblocks* principle can be applied and the obvious effect it has on actual customer service experiences. As you think about how you can apply this principle in your company, to inspire your employees to act like Rave, we've provided some strategies to assist you.

Remove the Roadblocks **Action Strategies**

- Anticipate a problem before it becomes a problem and take steps to avoid it.

- Train your employees on how to handle frequently asked questions so they're prepared to answer them.

- Cross-train your employees so if an employee is out sick, their job will still be done and it won't affect customers.

- Empower your employees with the knowledge and authority they need to take care of customers.

- Coach your employees for success. Give immediate feedback when they demonstrate an action or behavior that contributes to removing roadblocks.

Call to Action

What action steps can I take to bring this principle to life in my company?

1. _____

   _____

   _____

   _____

   _____

2. _____

   _____

   _____

   _____

   _____

3. _____

   _____

   _____

   _____

   _____

~ 1 ~

Think Like An Owner

~ 2 ~

Build a Relationship

~ 3 ~

Remove the Roadblocks

Principle Four:

Walk in Your Customer's Shoes

"Here is a simple but powerful rule: always give people more than what they expect to get."

Nelson Boswell, author, Inner Peace, Inner Power

Principle Four: Walk in Your Customer's Shoes

We've all heard the expression about walking a mile in someone else's shoes, but how often do we think about this concept when dealing with our customers? We often get so caught up in "doing our job" that we're too busy to really understand how our customers may feel.

The one thing everyone reading this book has in common is that we're all customers ourselves. As customers, we have our own expectations and needs that must be met for us to want to do business with a company. Too often, we don't think about what it's like to walk in our customers' shoes when we're taking care of them.

Think about what you want when you're a customer; your customers probably want the very same things you do. It's not too surprising that there are universal truths when it comes to customer service. Most customers want to be promptly taken care of by courteous, helpful and knowledgeable employees. As service providers, it's important to continually walk in your customers' shoes to better understand them and give them what they want. Otherwise, they won't be inspired to do business with you.

What do we mean by "walk in your customer's shoes"? Our definition is *to think about your customer, what he wants and how he wants to be treated.*

Have you ever put on your customers' shoes? We don't mean literally, of course, but figuratively. Once you do, ask yourself how it feels to be a customer of your organization. Good, bad or ugly...it's a vital exercise on the journey to become a more customer-centric organization.

The Importance of Touch Points

You and your employees have numerous opportunities to make impressions on potential, existing and former customers through touch points. These are all the interactions — direct and indirect — customers experience over the lifetime of their relationship with your company.

Touch points include your ads, website, salespeople, customer service representatives, store or office; they all affect the cumulative experience customers have with your company. Each of these touch points helps shape customers' perceptions of your company, generating one of three feelings: good, bad or indifferent.

Employee interactions are the most obvious touch points, but there are additional ways to learn how customers feel about your company. Surveys, focus groups and social media sites can be used to gather valuable feedback that can provide you with insight on how customers are being treated and, more importantly, how they want to be treated. Periodically evaluating your customers' experiences will uncover opportunities for improvement.

You may decide to make changes in the way you operate your business based on what you learn, changes that could have a positive effect on your customers' experiences. That could lead to additional revenue, more referrals, and higher customer retention. If you continually practice putting yourself in your customers' shoes and ask what motivates your customers to do business with your company and what makes your customers happy, you'll build a stronger customer-centric organization.

Gold or Platinum?

For many employees and companies, the Golden Rule continues to be a trusted approach to customer service: *Treat others as you would want to be treated.* However, the Platinum Rule is more effective when it comes to taking care of your customers: *Treat others the way **they** want to be treated.* Striving to understand what customers want from their perspective, not yours, is what it takes to deliver the Platinum Rule.

Most people have been conditioned to see things through their own eyes and how they act is based on those perceptions. While there is value to the Golden Rule, your customers have a different frame of reference and their own point of view. The key to earning customer loyalty is your ability to increase your awareness and see things from their perspective. Sometimes, we become so focused on all the tasks that need to get done at work that we lose sight of our customers' perceptions and forget that there's a human being on the other end of the phone or other side of the counter.

When applying this principle, we want you to think about "walking" through a customer's entire experience with your company, from the first phone call and uncovering the customer's need to the sale and the service after the sale. Every interaction and experience customers have with your company forms an impression in their mind of whether or not you can relate to their situation. This impression will dictate their buying decisions, so practicing this principle will help form more positive impressions with every customer interaction.

What Would Rant Do?

What came to mind when you read this comic strip? Are you concerned that this may be how employees behave in your business?

There are specific behaviors associated with the *Walk in Your Customer's Shoes* principle. It's important to identify the ones you don't want your employees displaying with your customers.

The list of negative behaviors (actions Rant might take) will help raise your awareness and define your expectations with your employees.

Here are the behaviors and actions that might be displayed when an employee like Rant is taking care of customers:

- *Not expressing empathy*

  Example: Not acknowledging when customers appear to be upset

- *Being insensitive to customers' situations*

  Example: Blaming customers rather than trying to help them

- *Being indifferent toward customers*

  Example: Not asking customers if you can help them

- *Not being considerate of customers*

  Example: Leaving customers on hold for extended periods of time

Later in this chapter, we'll contrast these behaviors with those an employee like Rave might display with customers.

Reality Check: United Airlines

Many real-life experiences have become timeless examples of poor customer service, like musician Dave Carroll's experience with United Airlines. Hell hath no fury like a musician scorned, as United Airlines discovered in 2009 when one of its baggage handlers destroyed a guitar as its owner looked on from inside the plane.

Dave became enraged when his numerous struggles to have United accept responsibility for the $1,200 in damage failed. When his frequent calls to United customer service representatives became futile, Dave put his songwriting skills to use. He penned a clever and catchy song describing his nine-month ordeal condemning the airline for the situation.

"You broke it, you should fix it. You're liable, just admit it. I should've flown with someone else. Or gone by car," Dave sings.

The video based on the song, which was seen by more than four million people within a month of being posted on YouTube, now has garnered more than 12 million views since debuting in 2010. It did more than just damage United's reputation; according to Chris Ayers of *The Times Online* in the United Kingdom, the incident cost the airline tens of millions of dollars.

"Within four days of the song going online, the gathering thunderclouds of bad PR caused United Airlines' stock price to suffer a mid-flight stall, and it plunged by 10 percent, costing shareholders $180 million. Which, incidentally, would have bought Dave more than 51,000 replacement guitars," Ayers wrote.

This blatant example of poor customer service clearly represents what not to do on so many levels, from the baggage handler's actions to the company's lack of response. The bad PR that resulted had enormous financial consequences to the company.

What was clearly lacking was empathy for the customer's feelings, a proactive approach to helping the customer and a genuine concern for his personal property. In this particular situation, we see the powerful effect of customers using social media to share their negative experiences. In fact, according to Forrester Technographics 2010 Customer Experience Online Survey, 24% of consumers who had unsatisfactory service interactions shared their experiences through social networks, a 50% increase over 2009.

Use this story as a reference point as you think about your own company and what you would have done differently if you'd been taking care of this customer.

Time for Reflection

Take time to think about your actions, and those of your employees, and answer the question below.

What behaviors are your employees demonstrating related to the *Walk in Your Customer's Shoes* principle that could be negatively affecting your Four Rs (revenue, retention, referrals and reputation)?

_____

_____

_____

_____

_____

_____

Making a Difference

If you and your employees practice this principle consistently, it will give you a competitive advantage. This can become your differentiator in a crowded or highly saturated marketplace, and especially during distressful times or slow economic periods. The most powerful aspect of this principle is that you can literally change the way someone is feeling.

Just imagine the difference for Dave Carroll if the baggage handler and the leaders at United Airlines had walked in his shoes. The outcome of the story would have been different; it would have had a better ending both for the customer and the company. Carroll's guitar would have safely made the trip, and United wouldn't have suffered the significant financial losses and damage to its reputation.

In the overcrowded, expensive airline industry, customers won't think twice about using a competitor because of poor service. According to the current Harris Interactive Customer Experience Impact Report, 89% of consumers quit doing business with a company because of a bad customer experience, up 59% from four years ago. This data points to the importance of understanding what the cost can be if you're not walking in your customers' shoes.

What Would Rave Do?

Clearly Rave's behavior—which reflects walking in the customer's shoes—contrasts drastically from Rant's.

Here are the behaviors and actions that might be displayed when an employee like Rave is taking care of customers:

- *Demonstrating sensitivity to customers' situations*
  Example: Acknowledging customers' feelings

- *Being proactive to help customers*
  Example: Offering to research alternative solutions for customers

- *Reassuring customers that you can help them*
  Example: Telling customers, "I see you're frustrated; let me help you"

- *Treating customers the way they want to be treated*
  Example: Asking customers what they'd like us to do for them

An Employee's Perspective

We know you're curious to read what an actual employee who displays these behaviors thinks about customer service and specifically this principle. The following insight from Megan Patz, an inbound sales and technical support representative for Go Daddy, is something to share with your employees, as they may be able to relate to her.

Megan has been employed with Go Daddy for nine months. Her phenomenal customer service skills have helped shape her reputation within the organization in that short amount of time. Megan is valued and admired for both her performance and her customer service beliefs.

"My personal philosophy on customer service is to take care of the customer," Megan said. *"The customer is priority one and we want to do what's best for the customer. That's the main goal. The customer is why I'm here, so to help them, whether it's to do something simple on their account or to discuss their business plans, my personal philosophy is that I want to help them succeed in their business and actually accomplish what they're trying to do.*

"A lot of it is ending the call on a good note," she continued. *"Hearing the customer say, 'That was a lot easier than I thought it would be' or 'It helped so much to have you walk me through that.' Getting the verbal feedback is great. We also send out customer satisfaction surveys. We look at those and our managers see them as*

well, so knowing our scores and what people think has an impact on your day."

Megan understands how important it is to listen. She eagerly wants to help her customers come to a resolution. Her attitude regarding customer service is uplifting and inspirational.

"We're here for the customer," Megan pointed out. *"Number one, that's our job. But hearing that satisfaction and hearing how much you've helped someone is great; it improves your day and makes you feel better about your job. It makes you successful at what you do and also makes the person you're helping more successful at what they're doing."*

Megan believes she and the Go Daddy team are very focused on walking in their customers' shoes.

"Most important, is putting the customer at ease. You want to put yourself in their position," she said. *"It's a combination of both removing the roadblocks and walking in your customer's shoes. You're definitely walking in their shoes so you understand where they're coming from and also how to support them in the changes or in the technical things that need to be done, while removing the roadblocks is to understand their technical level of understanding and kind of how to go about walking them through that. If they're very quick on the technical speak and they know what they're doing, what*

information can I give them that's blocking what they're trying to do? It's really about understanding what the problem is."

Rant or Rave?

There's a stark contrast between Megan and Go Daddy's philosophy on customer service and the baggage handler at United Airlines and what appears to be a lack of a customer service focus on the part of the United team. Megan's comment about putting customers at ease and putting herself in their position reinforces the value of this principle and demonstrates what you can expect from employees who practice it.

Do you have employees like Megan who demonstrate the behaviors associated with this principle? Do you have a customer service philosophy that reinforces this principle? As you contemplate these questions, remember the consequences of employees behaving like Rant and how they affect your opportunity to earn customers' loyalty.

Time for Reflection

Take a few minutes to think about your actions, and those of your employees, and answer the questions below.

What behaviors are your employees practicing related to the *Walk in Your Customer's Shoes* principle that could positively affect your Four Rs (revenue, retention, referrals and reputation)?

_____

_____

_____

_____

_____

_____

When you think about the behaviors you and your employees are currently displaying toward your customers with regard to walking in their shoes, are they more like Rant's or more like Rave's?

_____

_____

_____

_____

_____

_____

View from the Top

You've heard from an employee about the importance of walking in your customers' shoes. Now let's hear from a business owner.

Folkes Heating and Cooling in Fishkill, New York seems to have set up its own system when it comes to providing exceptional customer service. Employees "live" the company's main focus—building relationships and walking in their customers' shoes—with each and every customer they serve. Doing business with Folkes is not just about getting a unit fixed; it's about the quality of the entire experience.

"Say we go to a service call; our office calls before and says, 'Kurt is on his way,'" explained owner Dustin Folkes. *"He shows up and asks, 'Can I park in the driveway?' Before walking into the home, he puts on booties over his shoes and says, 'OK, I'm here to do an AC checkup, so I'll be in the basement.' This lets customers know what's going on, that he's not just walking around the house."*

Folkes aims to continually inform customers what's going on, keeping them involved in the whole experience. He refuses to have his customers confused or searching for answers; for the most part, customers should feel as though they have the advantage. To solidify this, customers receive follow-up calls a week or two after the service, asking how everything was and what could be improved. Technicians are also asked to leave surveys at customers' homes upon completion of projects.

"I use the Walmart mentality," Folkes said. *"It's not about what I want. Why should the customer get penalized? We offer service when it's convenient for them and not for us. When I'm home, I take my shoes off when I walk in my door. I wouldn't expect someone who's coming to work on my AC or stove to just walk in like they own the house and have no respect for my floors. That's why we have the booties."*

New Folkes employees are educated on how exceptional customer service is part of the company's philosophy and how very important it is. Employees who answer the phones in the office are required to have regular phone training and technicians are reminded about the importance of customer service during every company meeting.

"Our mission statement is to get customers and keep customers for life by providing outstanding service and exceeding customer expectations one hundred percent of the time," Folkes proudly stated. *"That's the culture I try to promote with my employees. Without the customers, we have no business."*

When you look at Folkes' comments in combination with Megan's, it's easy to see how the *Walk in Your Customer's Shoes* principle can be applied and the obvious effect it has on the actual customer experience. As you think about how to apply this principle in your company, to ensure you have a team of employees who act like Rave, we've provided some strategies to assist you.

Walk in Your Customer's Shoes **Action Strategies**

- Go through the steps potential customers would go through when attempting to do business with your company.

- Instruct your employees to acknowledge customers' feelings and teach them how to demonstrate empathy.

- Practice the Platinum Rule; treat your customers the way they want to be treated.

- Implement service standards and hold employees accountable for meeting them.

- Coach your employees for success. Give immediate feedback when they demonstrate an action or behavior that contributes to walking in your customer's shoes.

Call to Action

What action steps can I take to bring this principle to life in my company?

1. _____

_____

_____

_____

_____

2. _____

_____

_____

_____

_____

3. _____

_____

_____

_____

_____

~ 1 ~

Think Like An Owner

~ 2 ~

Build a Relationship

~ 3 ~

Remove the Roadblocks

~ 4 ~

Walk in Your Customer's Shoes

Principle Five:

Capture Your Customer's Heart

"When the customer comes first, the customer will last."

Robert Half, founder, Robert Half International

Principle Five: Capture Your Customer's Heart

Think about the last time someone captured your heart and how special and important that person made you feel. Imagine your customers feeling that way about you, your employees and *your* company.

An undeniable feeling occurs when your employees make your customers feel special. Ordinary experiences are turned into extraordinary ones, and customers are provided with magical and memorable moments.

When you think about companies that are known for capturing their customers' hearts and turning them into loyal brand advocates, which ones come to mind? For us, it's companies like Apple, Zappos and the Ritz Carlton; their customers are often loyal fans who share their passion for the company with anyone who'll listen. These companies are often equally recognized for the experience they provide their customers *and* their products or services.

What do we mean by "capture your customer's heart"? Our definition is to *create an emotional connection with your customer that makes him feel special and appreciated.*

Many customer service experiences don't involve any element of emotion or feeling conveying that the employees serving customers actually care about what they want or need. What's so amazing is that the things that make service experiences extraordinary are really quite simple, yet they can make customers feel so special.

Every interaction has two dimensions, human and business. The human dimension involves your emotions and interpersonal skills (listening, empathy, demonstrating appreciation, sympathy, acts and gestures of kindness and caring), while the business dimension involves your technical or task skills (problem-solving, asking questions, follow-up, product knowledge). We often focus more on the business dimension—completing the task at hand—yet it takes both skill sets to care for your customers and capture their hearts.

Did you know that Talbots, a women's retailer with 580 stores in 47 states, sends a birthday card to all its customers along with a special discount coupon to use during the month they were born? You don't have to be a company of Talbots' size to do this. Bella Luci, a hair salon in Poughkeepsie, New York, sends postcards to its clients to acknowledge birthdays. The owner of the Healey Brothers dealership in Beacon, New York calls his customers to wish them a happy birthday. Sal Ferro, President of Alure Home Improvements in Plainview, New York, throws customer appreciation parties each year. These types of gestures make customers feel special and appreciated. Any type or size business can capture their customers' hearts. Customers who feel a special connection will return for additional products and services and make referrals.

Small Acts of Kindness

Many businesses perform small acts of kindness. Some specific examples include sending customers thank-you cards after they make referrals, recognizing special events with handwritten notes congratulating them on wedding announcements or the birth of a child, and sending sympathy cards to acknowledge family deaths. These small acts of kindness build an emotional connection with your customers that will make them feel valued and appreciated.

Actions may speak louder than words, but never discount the importance of your employees' interpersonal skills. How they communicate during interactions may or may not create an emotional connection with customers.

What Would Rant Do?

What came to mind when you read this comic strip? Are you concerned that this may be how employees behave in your business?

There are specific behaviors associated with the *Capture Your Customer's Heart* principle. It's important to identify the ones you don't want your employees displaying with your customers.

The list of negative behaviors (actions Rant might take) will help raise your awareness and define your expectations with your employees.

Here are the behaviors and actions that might be displayed when an employee like Rant is taking care of customers:

- *Using tone of voice and body language that reflects insincere gratitude or lack of appreciation*

  Example: Sounding like you're reading from a script

- *Not relating to customers' concerns or situations*

  Example: Making inappropriate comments after customers have described their circumstances to you

- *Telling customers they're not important*

  Example: Saying, "I have other customers to take care of"

- *Insulting customers with actions or words*

  Example: Raising your voice with customers

Later in this chapter, we'll contrast these behaviors with those an employee like Rave might display with customers.

Lack of Human Dimension

Unfortunately, lack of empathy or human dimension is alive and well in many companies. This type of negative behavior often takes the spotlight on social media platforms that highlight customers' negative experiences. The example we're about to share is especially disturbing because of the unfortunate circumstances surrounding the customer's situation.

According to an NBC investigative report, friends of a Chicago man who lost nearly everything in an apartment fire took to Facebook, Twitter and Tumblr in a show of force against DirecTV after the company refused to budge on its early-termination policy.

The electrical fire that ravaged Bill Stern's apartment left his living room charred and his electronics melted, including the DirecTV satellite dish erected above his balcony.

He had many worries, but he didn't think canceling his DirecTV service, which he could no longer use, was one of them.

"Please help me," Bill recalled saying while pleading with the company. *"There's got to be someone there who can."*

To his dismay, the provider stood firm on the disconnection fee, which in Stern's case was $220.

"The supervisor said, 'We cannot cancel your service,' and I said, 'No, you won't cancel my service. Please help me,' and she said, 'No, we can't.'"

As he rebuilt his life from the rubble, Bill frequently fielded requests from friends asking how they could help—and that sparked an idea. *"I thought, 'Well, this is how you can help. You can Tweet and Facebook message DirecTV,'"* Bill explained.

Thus began the social media storm. Bill's friends pitched messages directly to and at the provider. Eventually, DirecTV did waive the $220 fee, but they declined to comment as to whether the social media messages played a part.

How would your employees have handled this situation? Do your employees make emotional connections with your customers or do they behave in ways that erode relationships, and are even insulting? Do you have policies that can destroy relationships and in turn damage your reputation?

After having a bad customer service experience in the past year, four out of five (80%) U.S. consumers told the people around them, many sharing their bad experiences via social media, according to the latest edition of an annual consumer behavior study by Accenture. This is a strong reminder that a good reputation is hard to earn, but easy to lose.

Time for Reflection

Take time to think about your actions, and those of your employees, and answer the question below.

What behaviors are your employees demonstrating related to the *Capture Your Customer's Heart* principle that could be negatively affecting your Four Rs (revenue, retention, referrals and reputation)?

_____

_____

_____

_____

_____

What Would Rave Do?

There's an obvious difference in Rave's interpersonal skills and how she communicates in this comic strip compared to Rant's approach. You'll also notice a clear difference in body language and the emotional connection that's made.

Here are the behaviors and actions that might be displayed when an employee like Rave is taking care of customers:

- *Making customers feel special*

  Example: Sending handwritten cards thanking them for their business

- *Personalizing customer experiences*

  Example: Using customers' names or remembering them from a previous interaction

- *Exceeding customer expectations*

  Example: Arranging for customers to get orders before they expect them

- *Being genuinely interested in customers*

   Example: Acknowledging special events like birthdays or awards

A Heartwarming Example: Panera Bread

As previously documented, customer service stories that go viral on the Internet often highlight negative experiences. Not so for a young man in Wilton, New Hampshire, Brandon Cook, who posted this heartwarming story on his Facebook wall about the customer service at Panera Bread in Nashua, New Hampshire.

"My grandmother is passing soon with cancer. I visited her the other day and she was telling me about how she really wanted soup, but not hospital soup, because she said it tasted like 'sh**'. She went on about how she really would like some clam chowder from Panera Bread. Unfortunately, it only sells clam chowder on Friday. I called the store and spoke with a manager, Sue, telling her the situation. I wasn't looking for anything special, just a bowl of clam chowder. Without hesitation, she said absolutely she'd make her some clam chowder. When I went to pick up it up, they wound up giving me a box of cookies as well. It's not that big of a deal to most, but to my grandma it meant a lot. I really want to thank Sue and the rest of the staff from Panera Bread just for making my grandmother happy. Thank you so much!"

This example of exceptional customer service not only captured Brandon's heart, it captured more than a half million hearts with a staggering 500,000 likes and 22,000 comments on Brandon's Facebook page. Additionally, Panera Bread's Facebook page was deluged with other people thanking the brand for the actions of one store manager.

An Employee's Perspective

Bernadette Mangione, an office manager at the Center for Dental Excellence in Hopewell Junction, New York, has been recognized for demonstrating exceptional customer service in every position she's held. Since she started working, all of Bernadette's positions required that she work with the public, and each employer has taken notice of the fact that Bernadette continually goes above and beyond what's expected of her.

"Whether or not the customer is always right, there's a way to make the customer think they are right," explained Bernadette. *"You need to diffuse whatever they're feeling with empathy. You can't be judging people. You can't predetermine a situation. You have to literally listen to a situation and want to cater to the customer. I try to put myself in their place and identify how I would want somebody to handle me in that situation."*

While speaking of her experiences with customer service, there was an obvious passion within Bernadette. She continually aims to please, wants to help and is genuinely focused on making her customers happy.

"I love to make people happy, I'm a people pleaser," Bernadette cheerfully stated. *"I want to turn around any situation and make the person walk away happy from it. I guess that's really the bottom line."*

In addition to wanting to make people happy, Bernadette is selfless in her customer service performance. She's not particularly concerned with recognition nor is she looking to be praised by customers. She believes there's a certain desire you must have to deliver exceptional customer service, and it, along with empathy, is its foundation.

In her current position, Bernadette goes out of her way to make sure patients are greeted warmly. She always remembers their names and includes handwritten notes in their bills, thanking them for being a patient or wishing them a happy holiday. "Bern," as she's known in the office, even delivered an envelope to a patient's home when it was returned for insufficient postage; it's this type of kindness and genuine interest in patients that creates opportunities to capture their hearts.

Rant or Rave?

You read how Sue made a customer's day at Panera Bread and how Bernadette prides herself on making her customers happy. Contrast this winning combination with the DirecTV employee who didn't demonstrate empathy and didn't make an emotional connection with the customer. You can see that capturing your customer's heart, combined with taking action, is a winning combination for your customers, your company and your Four Rs.

Time for Reflection

Take a few minutes to think about your actions, and those of your employees, and answer the questions below.

What behaviors are your employees practicing related to the *Capture Your Customer's Heart* principle that could positively affect your Four Rs (revenue, retention, referrals and reputation)?

_____

_____

_____

_____

_____

When you think about the behaviors you and your employees are currently displaying toward your customers, are they more like Rant's or more like Rave's?

_____

_____

_____

_____

_____

_____

View From The Top

Ken Berisha is one of the principals at the aforementioned Brother's Trattoria Italian restaurant. Aside from its delicious entrees, the establishment offers a warm, inviting atmosphere that keeps its customers not only well fed, but eager to return.

"You always have to treat a customer like they are a part of the family," shared Berisha, *"not just a number."*

It's no surprise with a philosophy like Berisha's that diners at Brother's find relaxation and comfort are part of their experience. This simple concept is supported by employee training conducted by either Berisha or his maître d', Jeff. As new employees are trained on restaurant operations, they are also introduced to the customer service philosophy of the restaurant. It's simply not just greeting customers; it's about making customers feel as though they're at home. Servers are taught to introduce themselves to their customers which makes it a more intimate connection.

The Maître d's Perspective

"Dealing with the public, you have to be an extrovert," said Jeff Polanco, Brother's maître d'. *"How you speak to the customers goes a long way."*

Jeff described Brother's as *"an escape, a getaway, where you always, always want to make the customer feel at home and part of the family."* He's warm, welcoming and rather observant to help his customers feel as comfortable as he can.

"All the details you pick up on, such as reading their body language and seeing how they're dressed, tell you more about that particular person so you can open up a conversation," Jeff said.

He offered a few examples of what works for him. For example, if a customer walks in wearing a Yankees t-shirt, Jeff asks about the latest game. If a woman is wearing a "#1 Mom" necklace, Jeff asks how many children she has. He even makes an effort to mention when he notices that a regular customer has a new hairstyle or recent haircut.

"It gets their attention. They say to themselves, 'Hey, someone noticed,'" believes Jeff. *"It leaves an impression giving them a special feeling that gets tied to the location."*

Motivating his employees takes place on a daily basis during the brief meetings he conducts before shifts start. They determine which wines to offer with which entrees, and Jeff also tends to ask his employees questions, such as, *"If you came into the restaurant, how would you like to be treated or spoken to? Make them ask, what's so great about this place?"*

Customer experiences in their restaurant are crucial. If customers feel as though they're being treated special, they become more loyal and are more likely to return.

"It's beyond the food," explained Jeff. *"It's about making the customer feel like a king or queen for the day. It's about making the customer feel like family from the moment they walk in to the moment they leave."*

All our principles appealed to Jeff, but the one that stuck out was *Capture Your Customer's Heart.* Jeff is convinced that it implies an emotional attachment in which you'll get the sale, but more importantly, earn a loyal repeat customer.

"The restaurant, bar, club atmosphere is an escape. It's an escape from the regular nine-to-five. When they come to the restaurant, it's their weekly affordable escape," Jeff noted. *"Once people know you remembered their first name, what they eat, the names of their children, or their issues, you start to touch them. That's where you're capturing their heart. It's all about the customer."*

Brother's Trattoria provides a good example of what it means to deliver exceptional customer service starting from the top. We see this through the owner's philosophy on customer service and how he instills his values and expectations within his employees. As you think about how to apply this principle in your company, to ensure you have a team of employees who act like Rave, we've provided some strategies to assist you.

Capture Your Customer's Heart **Action Strategies**

- Inspire your employees to exceed customer expectations.

- Provide ongoing training that will enhance employees' interpersonal communication skills.

- Challenge your employees to create their own list of "small acts of kindness."

- Evaluate your policies and make appropriate changes to prevent destroying customer relationships and damaging your company's reputation.

- Coach your employees for success. Give immediate feedback when they demonstrate an action or behavior that contributes to capturing your customer's heart.

Call to Action

What action steps can I take to bring this principle to life in my company?

1. _____

   _____

   _____

   _____

   _____

2. _____

   _____

   _____

   _____

   _____

3. _____

   _____

   _____

   _____

   _____

~ 1 ~

Think Like An Owner

~ 2 ~

Build a Relationship

~ 3 ~

Remove the Roadblocks

~ 4 ~

Walk in Your Customer's Shoes

~ 5 ~

Capture Your Customer's Heart

The Journey Continues

"When you serve the customer better, there's always a return on your investment."

Kara Parlin, copywriter, Hasbro Toys

The Journey Continues

We hope you enjoyed meeting Rant and Rave, and found the contrast in their behavior helpful as you recognize ways to relate it to your business. Our purpose in highlighting companies that deliver good customer service as well as those that don't was to show you that with good intentions, you can create better service experiences while learning from both types of situations.

We trust the excerpts from interviews with CEOs, business owners and employees gave you a broader range of knowledge and insight than you previously had. The statistics we shared should remind you of just how significant the financial consequences can be—good and bad—from providing or failing to provide exceptional customer service; your Four Rs are directly affected by the experiences customers have with you and your employees.

This chapter is designed to challenge you to continually strive to provide exceptional service experiences and exceed your customers' expectations. If you haven't completed the reflection exercises throughout the book, now is a good time to go back and work through them. If you have completed them, your responses will serve as a starting point to begin the next phase of your journey, which is to apply what you've learned in your own organization. We call it a journey because as you know, customer service isn't a destination, and delivering outstanding customer experiences is an ongoing process that requires persistent attention, constant evaluation and a dedicated effort to continually improve.

Paula Young, owner of Paula's Stone Cottage Wine Bar in Fishkill, New York, described her service journey like this: *"It's not about making a dollar, but making a customer. Make them feel that they mean something, that they matter. People can stay home and drink wine. They want an experience and we strive to give it to them."*

Practicing the five principles, along with implementing our strategies, will create a philosophy and core set of behaviors that can serve as a framework to get you started. This is your journey, so you need to decide exactly what you want or need to change and what you should be doing differently.

Remember, having a customer service strategy is a business imperative, not an option. In the high-stakes business world we live in, where change and competition are a constant, delivering quality customer service will continue to be the best business strategy to a thriving, successful company with loyal customers.

The "High-Stakes" of Customer Service

According to the 2012 American Express Global Customer Service Barometer, the company's annual survey of worldwide consumers, customer service is hugely influential with respect to customer preferences—especially when those customers are social media users. It proves once and for all that customer service—whether performed via social media or in-person—isn't simply a cost center; it's a way to reach new customers, earn more loyalty from the ones you already have, and boost revenue. Providing quality customer service is the best way to succeed in the high-stakes modern business world.

The survey painted a picture of consumers fed up with being on the receiving end of poor customer service practices, as evidenced in these customer service statistics:

- 93% of Americans say that businesses don't exceed their customer service expectations

- 80% of social media users have bailed on a purchase due to poor customer service, as have 55% of consumers overall

As you can see, consumers' expectations are not being met, and businesses are actually losing money as a result. The issue, however, simply isn't that poor customer service will hurt your business; it's that good customer service will greatly benefit your business, as evidenced by the same customer service barometer:

- Social media users are willing to pay 22% more for exemplary customer service, while the general population on average will pay about 13% more.

- American consumers who use social media for customer service will tell three times as many as those who don't.

This data reminds us that providing quality customer service isn't simply nice to have, especially when you look at how it affects your Four Rs. It validates that providing outstanding customer service is a way to grow *revenue*, increase customer *retention*, strengthen your *reputation* and give your customers a reason to make *referrals*.

Social Media—The New Word of Mouth

Given the increasing influence of social media on your business, we know you're aware that delighting customers is more important than it's ever been before. The American Express Customer Service Barometer shows that customers who use social media have higher customer service expectations.

Social media is the modern-day "word of mouth" and it's extremely powerful. What was previously a one-on-one interaction between customer and company now turns into a public dialogue when customers communicate their stories via social media sites such as Facebook, Twitter and YouTube. There are also review sites such as TripAdvisor.com, Yelp.com and Angieslist.com that up the ante on service expectations and can either bolster or ruin a company's reputation. Your prospective customers are reviewing those sites when deciding which companies to use. They have so many choices and they often make their buying decisions based on the comments they read—and if those comments are negative, that translates into a lost business opportunity for you.

According to ClickFox's 2011 Social Media for Customer Service Survey, word of mouth has a ripple effect on customers. More than 60% of customers are influenced or very influenced by other customers' comments about companies. Are you comfortable with what your customers are saying and sharing about their experiences with your company?

Sal Ferro of Alure Home Improvements takes word of mouth to a different level. He suggests closing your eyes and asking yourself, *"What do I want people to say about my business? You want your employees to say the same thing about your company that your customers say."* His company's vision statement is: *Deliver a consistent experience to our customers that is superior to what they expect.* Are you asking your employees what they would say about your business? And are they saying the same thing as your customers?

Rant or Rave?

As you observed the contrast in behaviors between Rant and Rave, some of you may have come to the sad realization that you have employees like Rant serving your customers. This is a good time to evaluate your team, discuss your service strategy and set expectations with your employees, as well as help them understand the effect they have on the customer's experience.

Our fictitious employees, Rant and Rave, can serve as benchmarks for behaviors to help your employees understand how their actions affect your Four Rs.

You know it's critical to hire the right people and have good systems and metrics in place. If you have discovered through this journey that you don't have the right people on your team, now is the time to act. If you have the right people, make sure you acknowledge their customer-focused behaviors.

What's Your Strategy?

Let's begin with a review of our five principles and their definitions:

1. Think Like an Owner

    Make decisions, solve problems and do what's right for customers as if you're the owner of the company.

2. Build a Relationship

    Establish rapport, demonstrate you care and show genuine interest in your customers and their needs.

3. Remove the Roadblocks

    Eliminate obstacles that get in the customer's way of doing business with you.

4. Walk in Your Customer's Shoes

    Think about your customer, what he wants and how he wants to be treated.

5. Capture Your Customer's Heart

    Create an emotional connection with your customer that makes him feel special and appreciated.

One or more of these principles may resonate with you and you may decide that it will become the core of your service strategy. During our interview with Lou DiFabio, Executive Vice President of Chemung Canal Trust Company, he commented on the use of the principles this way: *"I recognize the five principles of customer service and instinctively classified them into two 'buckets.' Thinking like an owner and removing the roadblocks are how you can empower your people to do the right thing. The other three, building a relationship, walking in your customer's shoes and capturing your customer's heart, are all about relationship building and empathy. Our objective is building a relationship."*

We recommend a three-step strategy to move forward:

- Refer to *Behaviors at a Glance* on page 145 for a list of the behaviors associated with each principle.

- Review your reflection pages and determine which of the principles you're already practicing and which you need to begin to apply in your business. Refer to page 143 for a list of *The Five Principles*.

- Select the strategies for the principles you want to focus on and take steps to put them into action. Refer to page 153 for a complete list of *Action Strategies* for each principle.

What's in Your Mirror?

What is the reflection in your mirror? Are you modeling the behaviors you want your employees demonstrating with your customers? The journey begins with you. Are you practicing the Platinum Rule with your employees? Are you treating them the way you want them to treat your customers?

Make your employees feel important (just as important as your customers) and let them know that they're valued members of your team. Eliminate roadblocks that get in the way of *them* delighting your customers. Work as hard to earn your employees' loyalty as you do to earn your customers' loyalty. When you do, it will inspire them to deliver exceptional customer experiences.

Rant discovered at the end of her journey that she's been turning off customers. What will you learn on yours, once you reflect on your own behavior and that of your employees? With a new level of awareness comes responsibility. We hope you'll share what you've learned with your employees and start a journey with them to create loyal customers who are inspired to rave about your company.

Here's to turning rants into raves!

The Five Principles

1. Think Like an Owner

   Make decisions, solve problems and do what's right for customers as if you're the owner of the company.

2. Build a Relationship

   Establish rapport, demonstrate you care and show genuine interest in your customers and their needs.

3. Remove the Roadblocks

   Eliminate obstacles that get in the customer's way of doing business with you.

4. Walk in Your Customer's Shoes

   Think about your customer, what he wants and how he wants to be treated.

5. Capture Your Customer's Heart

   Create an emotional connection with your customer that makes him feel special and appreciated.

Behaviors at a Glance

Think Like an Owner

Rant

- *Unnecessarily passing customers to another employee*
  Example: Referring customer to a co-worker rather than helping them

- *Not taking an interest in customers or their needs*
  Example: Ignoring customers when they need help

- *Trivializing customers' problems*
  Example: Telling customers, "I can't believe you're making a big deal about this"

- *Making customers feel like they're an interruption*
  Example: Rolling eyes and asking "Yes?" when customers approach them while they're speaking with another employee

Rave

- *Taking responsibility for customers even if it's not your job*
  Example: Processing a credit rather than transferring customers to the accounting department to have them do it

- *Doing whatever it takes to make sure customers are satisfied*
  Example: Answering customers' questions and confirming their needs were met

- *Making customers your top priority*
  Example: Giving customers your undivided attention

- *Resolving customers' problems even if you didn't cause them*
  Example: Telling customers, "I can take care of that for you"

Build A Relationship

Rant

- *Displaying negative body language*
  Example: Not maintaining eye contact or smiling when speaking with customers

- *Not greeting customers*
  Example: Saying "Next" versus "Good morning, how may I help you"?

- *Pushing products rather than asking questions to uncover customer needs*
  Example: Assuming they know what customers want without asking them

- *Acting disinterested in customers*
  Example: Not listening to customers and being

distracted by other employees, their cell phone or something else

Rave

- *Establishing rapport by acknowledging customers*
  Example: Asking for and using customers' names during conversations
- *Remembering customers*
  Example: Asking repeat customers about something they shared with you the last time you spoke to them
- *Thanking customers for their business*
  Example: Telling customers you appreciate them doing business with your company
- *Following up with customers*
  Example: Telling customers you'll call them back and then doing so

Remove the Roadblocks

Rant

- *Not demonstrating flexibility*
  Example: Telling a customer, "I can't help you. This is the company's policy."

- *Not demonstrating a willingness to help*

  Example: Not offering to help customers when the person they ask for isn't available

- *Asking for information that's already been provided*

  Example: Asking for customers' account numbers after they've been entered into your automated system

- *Not proactively communicating relevant information*

  Example: Not informing customers about pricing changes that affect them

Rave

- *Making it easy for customers*

  Example: Offering to look up information for customers rather than having them do it themselves

- *Demonstrating a sense of empowerment*

  Example: Making a decision you think your manager would make if he was faced with a similar situation

- *Telling customers what you can do*

  Example: Offering customers another option rather than telling them, "No, I can't"

- *Anticipating potential problems and taking steps to resolve them before they affect customers*

  Example: Proactively communicating a product is on backorder so customers can plan accordingly

Walk in Your Customer's Shoes

Rant

- *Not expressing empathy*

  Example: Not acknowledging when customers appear to be upset

- *Being insensitive to customers' situations*

  Example: Blaming customers rather than trying to help them

- *Being indifferent toward customers*

  Example: Not asking customers if you can help them

- *Not being considerate of customers*

  Example: Leaving customers on hold for extended periods of time

Rave

- *Demonstrating sensitivity to customers' situations*

  Example: Acknowledging customers' feelings

- *Being proactive to help customers*

  Example: Offering to research alternative solutions for customers

- *Reassuring customers that you can help them*

  Example: Telling customers, "I see you're frustrated; let me help you"

- *Treating customers the way they want to be treated*

  Example: Asking customers what they'd like us to do for them

Capture Your Customer's Heart

Rant

- *Using tone of voice and body language that reflects insincere gratitude or lack of appreciation*

  Example: Sounding like you're reading from a script

- *Not relating to customers' concerns or situations*

  Example: Making inappropriate comments after customers have described their circumstances to you

- *Telling customers they're not important*

  Example: Saying, "I have other customers to take care of"

- *Insulting customers with actions or words*

  Example: Raising your voice with customers

Rave

- *Making customers feel special*

  Example: Sending handwritten cards thanking them for their business

- *Personalizing customer experiences*

  Example: Using customers' names or remembering them from a previous interaction

- *Exceeding customer expectations*

  Example: Arranging for customers to get orders before they expect them

- *Being genuinely interested in customers*

  Example: Acknowledging special events like birthdays or awards

Action Strategies

Think Like an Owner Action Strategies

- Define what it means to you to serve customers and communicate that to your employees.

- Help your employees develop strong decision-making skills.

- Communicate what you expect your employees to do to serve customers in your absence.

- Establish what it means to go above and beyond customers' expectations.

- Coach your employees for success. Give immediate feedback when they demonstrate an action or behavior that contributes to thinking like an owner.

Build a Relationship Action Strategies

- Implement a service interaction model that includes building rapport.

- Strive to use customers' names 100% of the time.

- Establish a practice within in your organization to follow up with your customers.

- Thank your customers each and every time they do business with your company.

- Coach your employees for success. Give immediate feedback when they demonstrate an action or behavior that contributes to building a relationship.

Remove the Roadblocks **Action Strategies**

- Anticipate a problem before it becomes a problem and take steps to avoid it.
- Train your employees on how to handle frequently asked questions so they're prepared to answer them.
- Cross-train your employees so if an employee is out sick, their job will still be done and it won't affect customers.
- Empower your employees with the knowledge and authority they need to take care of customers.
- Coach your employees for success. Give immediate feedback when they demonstrate an action or behavior that contributes to removing roadblocks.

Walk in Your Customer's Shoes **Action Strategies**

- Go through the steps potential customers would go through when attempting to do business with your company.
- Instruct your employees to acknowledge customers' feelings and teach them how to demonstrate empathy

- Practice the Platinum Rule; treat your customers the way they want to be treated.

- Implement service standards and hold employees accountable for meeting them.

- Coach your employees for success. Give immediate feedback when they demonstrate an action or behavior that contributes to walking in your customer's shoes.

Capture Your Customer's Heart **Action Strategies**

- Inspire your employees to exceed customer expectations.

- Provide ongoing training that will enhance employees' interpersonal communication skills.

- Challenge your employees to create their own list of "small acts of kindness."

- Evaluate your policies and make appropriate changes to prevent destroying customer relationships and damaging your company's reputation.

- Coach your employees for success. Give immediate feedback when they demonstrate an action or behavior that contributes to capturing your customer's heart.

Sources

For the references cited throughout the book, the chapter name and a short phrase corresponding to each one are listed below.

The Journey Begins

Forrester Research, The State of the Customer Experience, 2012. Of all the businesses surveyed, 93% identified the customer experience among their strategic priorities, and 28% placed it at the top of the list. Additionally, 75% plan to use it as a key differentiator.

http://www.lithium.com/pdfs/whitepapers/lithium-state-of-customer-exp2012.pdf

American Express Global Customer Service Barometer. 78% of customers have bailed somewhere in the buying process because of poor customer service.

http://about.americanexpress.com/news/docs/2012x/AXP_2 012GCSB_Markets.pdf

Parature's customer service blog. Poor customer experiences result in an estimated $83 billion loss by U.S. enterprises each year because of defections and abandoned purchases.

http://www.parature.com/targeting-customer-experience-board-benefits/

The Research Institute of America (RIA). An average business will never hear a word from 96% of their unhappy customers whose complaints range from poor service, rudeness, to discourteous treatment.

http://www.serviceuntitled.com/category/customer-service/page/3/

Social Media for Customer Service Survey from ClickFox (2011). Word of mouth has a ripple effect on other customers. More than 60% of customers are influenced or very influenced by other customers' comments about companies.

http:// clickfox.com

General Services Administration (GSA). Workgroups with higher levels of engagement had, on average, 23% to 26% more highly satisfied and loyal customers, which equated to more than $1 million in revenue than workgroups with low or slightly engaged employees.

http://www.gallup.com/poll/7576/Federal-Agency-Explores-CustomerEmployee-Link.aspx

Harrah's Entertainment. Through the efforts of Nigel Martin, former VP of Leadership and Learning at Harrah's Entertainment (now Caesar's Entertainment Inc.), the company embarked on a two-year initiative to improve internal employee engagement.

http://www.danpontefract.com/can-employee-engagement-improve-customer-satisfaction

Think Like an Owner

The Wharton School's David Sirota and Louis Mischkind. Their findings are based on 30 years of research involving 2.5 million employees in 237 companies, organizations with high morale outperform their competitors by roughly 20%.

http://knowledge.wharton.upenn.edu/article.cfm?articleid=1188

Zappos story. I'm reminded of a time when I was in Santa Monica, California a few years ago at a Skechers sales conference. After a long night of barhopping, a small group of us headed up to someone's hotel room to order some food.

http://www.huffingtonpost.com/tony-hsieh/branding-through-customer_b_799316.html

Build a Relationship

TARP, the world's premier customer experience agency. Customer churn is caused by feelings of poor treatment 68% of the time.

http://www.tarp.com

RightNow Technologies Customer Experience Impact Report 2011. 50% of customers will give you one week to respond to a question before they stop doing business with you. http://www.rightnow.com/files/analyst-reports/RightNow_Customer_Experience_Impact_Report_North_America_2011.pdf

FedEx video. A hilariously sad video of a FedEx deliveryman chucking a computer monitor attracted nearly 200,000 views on YouTube in a single day. Many of those people expressed fears that their packages would be treated with the same disregard.

http://www.dailymail.co.uk/news/article-2076432/FedEx-guy-caught-throwing-monitor-fence-YouTube-video.html

ContactPoint Client Research. Sadly, employees only ask for the customer's name 21% of the time (the person has a name 100% of the time).

http://www.contactpoint.com

Remove the Roadblocks

Southwest Airlines. According to Sharmon Walters, Manager of Southwest's People Department, Southwest Airlines employees are empowered to make decisions that provide outrageous customer service, even if it's coloring outside the line of what's normally done.

http://talentmgt.com/articles/view/take-employer-branding-to-the-next-level/5

Corporate Executive Board Study. There's an 86% likelihood that customers will purchase products from companies that simplify the purchase journey.

http://img.en25.com/Web/CEB/MLC%20Decision%20Simpl icity%20Harvard%20Business%20Review%20Article.pdf

Stew Leonard's, a food and dairy store known for its exceptional service and named one of Fortune 100's Best Companies to Work 10 years in a row.

http://www.stewleonards.com

A recent Reuter's survey in *Consumer Reports*. The top three reasons causing telephone customer angst are not getting a human on the phone, too many phone steps, and a long wait on hold.

http://graphics.thomsonreuters.com/11/06/us_consammgst 0611_sc.gif

America Online found out how scripted customer service representatives can sound when a New York man recorded his attempt to cancel his service.

http://www.msnbc.msn.com/id/13447232/ns/business-cnbc_tv/t/how-hard-can-it-be-cancel-aol-account/#.UG85Jk01_ng

Nordstrom story. A Portland, Oregon man who needed an Armani tuxedo for his daughter's wedding, as a last-ditch effort to find the tuxedo, went to the local Nordstrom.

http://toddand.com/2007/02/18/legends-of-unbelievable-nordstrom-service/

Maritz Research study. Employees often feel their hands are tied by corporate policies that focus on bottom-line needs rather than those of the customers they're supposed to serve.

http://www.maritzresearch.com/employeeengagement-news.aspx

Walk in Your Customer's Shoes

United Airlines. Hell hath no fury like a musician scorned, as United Airlines discovered in 2009 when one of its baggage handlers destroyed a guitar as its owner looked on from inside the plane.

http://www.seoptimise.com/blog/2009/07/united-airlines-lose-millions-youtube.html

Forrester Technographics 2010 Customer Experience Online Survey. 24% of consumers who had unsatisfactory service interactions shared their experiences through social networks, a 50% increase over 2009.

http://forrester.com

Harris Interactive Customer Experience Impact Report. 89% of consumers quit doing business with a company because of a bad customer experience, up 59% from four years ago.

http://harrisinteractive.com

Capture Your Customer's Heart

An NBC investigative report. Friends of a Chicago man who lost nearly everything in an apartment fire took to Facebook, Twitter and Tumblr in a show of force against DirecTV after the company refused to budge on its early-termination policy.

http://www.nbcchicago.com/investigations/series/target-5/social-media-directv-bill-sterns-163639936.html

Accenture annual consumer behavior study. After having a bad customer service experience in the past year, four out of five (80%) U.S. consumers told the people around them, many sharing their bad experiences via social media.

http://www.accenture.com/us-en/Pages/insight-accenture-customer-satisfaction-survey-2010-summary.aspx?c=mc_othrposts_10000022&n=sm_0910

Panera Bread story. A young man in Wilton, New Hampshire, Brandon Cook, posted this heartwarming story on his Facebook wall about the customer service at Panera Bread in Nashua, New Hampshire.

http://news.yahoo.com/blogs/trending-now/panera-bread-gets-social-media-love-helping-dying-193201463.html

The Journey Continues

American Express Global Customer Service Barometer. Customer service is hugely influential with respect to customer preferences—especially when those customers are social media users.

http://about.americanexpress.com/news/docs/2012x/AXP_2012 GCSB_Markets.pdf

American Express Global Customer Service Barometer. Customers who use social media have higher customer service expectations.

http://about.americanexpress.com/news/docs/2012x/AXP_2 012GCSB_Markets.pdf

ClickFox's 2011 Social Media for Customer Service Survey. Word of mouth has a ripple effect on customers.

http://clickfox.com/

Tell Us Your Story

Do you have a customer service story you'd like to share with us? We're always interested in hearing about experiences other people have with employees like Rant or Rave. Your story could be in our next book!

Please send your story to info@turningrantsintoraves.com.

About the Authors

Randi Busse is President of Workforce Development Group, Inc., a training organization that partners with companies to improve customer service, increase customer retention, and maximize revenue through consultative selling and referrals. Since her company's inception, Randi has become a trusted resource for many diverse companies and organizations that have relied on her guidance to help improve the experience they're providing to their customers. Her programs foster a culture of ownership among employees and provide them with the skills they need to delight customers.

Randi earned an M.S. in Organizational Management from University of Phoenix. She's an engaging and inspiring speaker who uses real-life situations and humor to customize the content of her programs, getting you and your employees excited and motivated to turn your customers into loyal promoters of your company.

Contact Randi:

Workforce Development Group
randi@workdevgroup.com
631-598-5598

Carol Heady is President of Learning and Performance Solutions, a consulting and training company that helps organizations improve performance in two key areas: customer service and leadership. Carol is a trainer, consultant, facilitator, author, speaker and executive coach. She's trained thousands of employees to deliver customer service excellence, and coached hundreds of managers to increase their leadership effectiveness.

Carol works with clients to implement training programs and management reinforcement strategies that improve customer satisfaction, build customer loyalty, and increase revenue. Her leadership development programs focus on increasing self-awareness, team effectiveness, and building coaching competencies to maximize individual and organizational performance.

Carol earned an M.S. in Organizational Management and Human Resource Development from Manhattanville College, and received her coaching training from the leading global provider of coach training programs, Coach U.

Contact Carol:

Learning and Performance Solutions
carol@learningandperformancesolutions.com
845-226-8047

Services Offered

Carol and Randi offer a range of customized onsite programs, and are available for keynotes at conferences, association meetings, and trade shows. To learn more, visit our website at www.turningrantsintoraves.com or contact us at info@turningrantsintoraves.com.

Made in the USA
Charleston, SC
12 February 2014